J /

She Will *NOT* Grow Out Of It !
A Memoir of Love, Hope & Promise

By Pam Silverwood
With David B. Hack

May 5, 2017

Cover photo–Richard Lee Brawley
Cover design–David B. Hack

An Amazon Kindle Digital Publishing (KDP) Book
ISBN: 9781521083147

DavidBHack@yahoo.com

i 6 - 2 - 17

CONTENTS

PROLOGUE

"Good morning, Pam. The Commanding General wants to see you right away!"

"Oh, that's funny; you guys are *really good!*"

"Yes, we know. And you really *are* wanted in the General's office–STAT! Here's the message; you're excused from the staff meeting."

What could I have done? I thought minutes later, as I run-skittered through the polished hallways. *I can't have killed anyone! Speech therapy is not a lethal discipline!* This was my fourth year at Walter Reed Army Hospital; I had never been in the Commanding General's office for any reason. Called on the carpet now, without a clue, I was terrified. My feet were still racing my heart as I turned into the outer office....

"Yes, Miss Silverwood, you may go right in. Colonel Wilson[1] is with the General."

Omigod, my boss's boss's boss. I'm dead!

"Good morning, Pam. How are you today?"

"I'll know in a minute, Colonel Wilson." Looking back now, I wish I could say that I continued confidently: "Good morning, General Mahoney; why am I here?" But I felt like a sinner approaching St. Peter at the Pearly Gates. Whatever greeting I directed to the Commanding General, it was not with confidence...

---

[1] Col. Wilson is a pseudonym. I don't remember the name of my boss's boss's boss!

[2] Jack Anderson was a famous, muckraking, syndicated newspaper columnist, who worked out of Washington, D.C., cultivating a vast network of confidential informants, exposing every suggestion of

General Mahoney began: "Secretary Laird called me this morning from the Pentagon; he got a call from the White House. Are you seeing Senator Mundt as an outpatient?"

Oh, so that's it, I thought. Senator Mundt of South Dakota had suffered a stroke last year. I had been trying ever since to teach him to talk again. *Someone at the White House has called the Secretary of Defense about it. Senator Mundt's AA, or Mrs. Mundt, must be behind all this. Oh Lord, help me; I'm too young to die!*

"Yes, Sir—I *was*."

"Have you discharged him?"

"Yes, Sir."

"Can you tell me about that?"

My mind started racing, reeling....

***

A few days earlier, the Senator's Administrative Assistant, or "AA," had brought him to my office, as usual, for his therapy session. After the session, I had told the AA that I was discharging the Senator from treatment and told him why. His face fell. He said that they were planning to run the Senator for re-election, and added, "All we have to do is print his picture in the paper. He has been Senator for so long, he will win...."

"That would be wrong," I replied. "If you do that, I will have to go to Jack Anderson.[2]

---

[2] Jack Anderson was a famous, muckraking, syndicated newspaper columnist, who worked out of Washington, D.C., cultivating a vast network of confidential informants, exposing every suggestion of government misdeed in his column, "The Washington Merry-Go-

The AA continued: "...Mrs. Mundt wants the Senator to run for President."

***

"Miss Silverwood," repeated the General, "Can you tell me why you discharged Senator Mundt?"

"General Mahoney, I have been working with Senator Mundt now for half-a-year. He's made practically no progress, and none recently. Shortly after we started, he couldn't say anything but 'Chewdy, chewdy, chewdy.' He still can say nothing else. If I ask him 'Is it raining in this room?,' he smiles like I'm his best friend, pumps his head up and down and says 'Chewdy, chewdy, chewdy.' He's made no recent progress at all. Yes, Sir, I discharged him."

"You've exhausted every reasonable possibility?"

"Yes Sir. General, the wards are filled up with men back from Vietnam—some with wounds to the head and others with blood clots in the brain. I've got one man who has part of his head chopped off flat by a helicopter blade. His wife and her parents are coming to visit him this week, for the first time. I'd like nothing better than to be able to help Senator Mundt, but I'm only one person—the only speech pathologist working here at the main hospital building, with the inpatients. I'm staying some nights till 7 PM. Sir, if I see Senator Mundt once or twice a week, there is another wounded soldier here somewhere that I won't be able to see."

Round." He followed in the footprint of his late mentor, Drew Pearson. Before retiring, Jack Anderson won a Pulitzer Prize. He also mentored (and turned the syndicated column over to) Doug Cohn, who continued the tradition.

"Mmmm...Hmmm."

"But you're the commander, Sir. If you tell me to keep seeing Senator Mundt, I will do it. Just tell me what you want me to do."

"No, Miss Silverwood, you're doing the right thing. Keep doing as you're doing; I'll take care of the White House and Mrs. Mundt. Thank you for coming."[3]

---

[3] Karl E. Mundt of South Dakota served in the U.S. Senate from December 31, 1948 to Jan. 3, 1973 and in the House of Representatives from 1939 to 1948. In 1960, he ran successfully for re-election to the Senate against George McGovern, who was later the 1972 Democratic candidate for President. In 1972, Sen. Mundt did not run for re-election to the Senate (or for President), and he died August 16, 1974.

WALTER REED

I first heard about the Walter Reed Army Hospital when General Dwight Eisenhower was the President and confined there following abdominal surgery, for ileitis. It was June of 1956, and I was almost seventeen. Like my mother, I was fascinated with celebrities, and the President–the General, the Supreme Allied Commander, the leader who gave the "go" for D-Day in Word War II–was surely a celebrity. I had planned since the fourth grade to be a speech therapist, and more recently I had decided I wanted to do my speech therapy in a hospital setting. By the time I heard that the president was confined at Walter Reed Army Hospital, I was quite familiar with doctors and hospitals. Way *too* familiar in fact.

***

I'd had my first surgery the day I was born, to close up a hole in my spinal column that exposed my spinal cord to open view–open air–and the possibility of infection. I was born with Spina Bifida Myelo-meningocele, the worst degree of Spina Bifida.[4] Not only must the hole be closed, my parents were told, but I might need an operation on my skull to put in a

---

[4] Though I suppose the causes of Spina Bifida are still being studied, the most important factor seems to be an absence or insufficiency, before and during pregnancy, of a particular nutrient known as Folic Acid (also known as Vitamin B-9). It seems that experts are now recommending that every girl and woman of child-bearing age should take Folic Acid/Vitamin B-9 as a supplement, every day of their lives until menopause. If such a simple precaution truly can eliminate Spina Bifida, who wouldn't want to do that? I think every daily multivitamin formulation, certainly those marketed especially to women, should include this vital nutrient.

"shunt." Without a shunt to drain fluid from my brain, my head could swell up like a basketball, causing brain damage and eventual death. If death didn't follow, I was likely to be a near vegetable anyway; I would probably never walk or talk, and I would be mentally "handicapped." This gloomy prospect was sufficiently sobering to doctors that the surgeon who closed my lesion told my parents that they should immediately institutionalize me, before they got attached to me. Answering that, my father said, "No, she's part of our family. When she can leave the hospital, she's coming home with us."

I didn't walk until I was two. At five, I was clumping around in long leg casts, which were prescribed to correct my misaligned lower limbs.

Around the same age, my urologist, Doctor Huggins, did a "sympothectomy" to improve my bladder control. Whether it did or not, I don't know; I finally achieved fair control of my bladder when I was nine!

Dr. Huggins treated me throughout my child-hood, and he was very nice. He even once said to me, "If your parents ever get tired of you, you can always come and live with me." I knew that my parents would never get tired of me, but his words stayed with me right to this day. It was so nice and comforting to know that, if something ever happened to my parents, I always had a soft place to land.[5]

---

[5] Dr. Charles Brenton Huggins was awarded in 1966 the Nobel Prize for Physiology or Medicine–for discovering in 1941 that hormones could be used to control the spread of some cancers.

My Mom and Dad, striding out to see a movie, in celebration of my first baby steps that day at age two.

When I was fifteen, I was falling on the ice and snow, much more than other kids my age. So, I had an operation, on one foot—a "triple arthrodesis." Some doctor—as I was being wheeled in for surgery, and in response to my question–told me that the operation would enable me to wear high heels. He must have been making that up; the surgery didn't enable me to wear high heels. But it did improve my stability on ice and snow.

Following that surgery, I was very sick for months, with many bladder infections and terrible pain. This became such an issue that any thought of surgery on the other foot was forgotten, and it was never done. Finally, the doctors discovered that one of my kidneys was infected and not working, so that not only was it not helping me, it was poisoning my body every day of my life. Doctor Huggins told me, "If you can stand the pain of a kidney infection, you can stand the pain of childbirth."

So the kidney had to go. My mother exclaimed, one afternoon as she worried through a game of golf, "My God, they're going to cut her in half!"

Before the surgery to remove the kidney could occur, though, my pain became so intense that my family were themselves painfully aware of my distress and attentive to my moans and near-screams. My younger brother Jim, in particular, at ten years old, was extremely sweet to me. One day, he stayed by my bedside for hours–all day long, actually–holding my hand and speaking words of comfort. He would say, "When the pain is worst, squeeze my hand–as hard as you can–it's OK." He was ready to take on my pain–to feel it himself–to lessen mine. I've never forgotten his insistent and persistent caretaking in this, my time of greatest agony.

My surgeon for this operation was a Dr. Vermuelen. He didn't exactly cut me in half–he cut only half-way around my body—and he was nice enough to sew me up again.

The next morning, the nurses came in, all bright and cheery, saying, "We're going to get you up this morning—let you sit in the chair for a while." I said, "Oh, no! You don't want to do that! I can't do that!" "Oh, yes you can! We're going to help you." "Oh, I can't! If you get me up, I'm going to faint!" Well, they got me up, and they helped me over to the chair. And they sat me down, and—for the first time in my life—I fainted.

Later that day, they got me to walking. I was walking slowly down the corridor, all bent over toward my left side, where the stitches were. Who should come by just then but my old friend, my urologist Dr. Huggins, who had referred me to surgery. He saw me, all bent over toward the side, and he said, "Straighten up, Pam!" He took my shoulders in his hands, and he straightened me up. He *certainly* did! I immediately looked down, in a panic, *expecting to see all my insides fallen down to the floor!*

But I survived. Within days, I was saying, "Wow! Is this how I'm supposed to feel?" Waves of new energy were chasing through my teenaged body!

***

So when I heard about President Eisenhower's stay in the Walter Reed Army Hospital in Washington, D.C., I had some reason to sympathize with his situation; I'd had too much experience of hospitals, myself. Anyway, I well remembered the name of President Ike's hospital.

Most people then knew little of Walter Reed Army Hospital, perhaps having never heard of it. Many of our more recent Presidents have previously served in the *Navy*, and subsequently, as President, have had their annual checkups and occasional treatment at the *Naval* Hospital in Bethesda, Maryland.[6] Presidents Richard Nixon, Gerald Ford, Jimmy Carter, and George H.W. Bush come to mind as former *Navy* men. But "General Ike" was Army, and as President he chose to be treated at the Army's Walter Reed.

Walter Reed, the hospital, was named for the man. Perhaps when you were young, you read the book *Walter Reed, Doctor in Uniform*, or *The Doctors Who Conquered Yellow Fever,* or Paul DeKruif's 1926 Classic, *Microbe Hunters*. The hospital's namesake, in the years just following the Spanish American War in Cuba, was the leader of the Yellow Fever Commission, a group of Army doctors that was established by the Surgeon General of the Army to discover the cause of yellow fever and how to prevent it. One Cuban doctor, Dr. Carlos Juan Finlay, believed (quite alone) that the disease was transmitted by mosquitoes.

Daringly then, for their use of human test subjects, Reed and his colleagues used infected mosquitoes to prove (1) that a certain female mosquito was definitely the "vector" of transmission; (2) that each individual mosquito had to have bitten a yellow fever patient in his first few days of infection and then have passed through an incubation period before her bite would transmit the disease; and (3) that exposure to people sick with the fever, or to their soiled bed linen

---

[6] The Army and Navy hospitals eventually were merged into one *Military* hospital. See a subsequent footnote.

and such, was not (as previously thought) the cause of yellow fever.

One or two of the brave test subjects died; the others recovered. Dr. Reed had been ready to infect himself through mosquito bites, but others volunteered in his stead. The following year, 1902, Reed died of a burst appendix at 51, and the main Army hospital was subsequently named for him. But after Reed proved that the culprit was the mosquito, one of Reed's colleagues succeeded in ridding the Canal Zone in Panama of yellow fever (and also malaria), which enabled U.S. construction of the Panama Canal–contributing greatly to American military power and commerce in The American Century (the 20th) and down to this day.

Through the century, the hospital that became "Walter Reed" took and treated the most serious acute cases–active and retired soldiers, their dependents, Senators, Presidents and foreign dignitaries–in war and peace, through two world wars, Korea and beyond. At mid-century, Reed's memorial hospital sat at the pinnacle of Army (some say *military*) medicine. It was the training site that young Army doctors wanted to pass through and the prestige hospital where they might someday return, as senior administrators or celebrated military surgeons. It was the place where the soldiers most gravely wounded by war were sent for acute care before being transferred to other military or veterans hospitals, or discharged to home or back to their post. It was also a prestige job where a young speech-language pathologist could give something to her country and, in 1967, to those fighting a most controversial war in Vietnam.

Little did I know, thinking about President Eisenhower's illness in the summer of 1956, in my South Chicago home, that the President's hospital–Walter Reed Army Medical Center–was also in my future. [7] [8] [9]

[7] "The Founding of Walter Reed General Hospital and the Beginning of Modern Institutional Army Medical Care in the United States," http://jhmas.oxfordjournals.org/content/69/4/521 Retrieved November 15, 2015.

[8] In 2011, Walter Reed Army Medical Center and the National Naval Medical Center in Bethesda, Maryland, were merged. The combined facility is located in Bethesda and known as the Walter Reed National Military Medical Center.

[9] Ironically, after I got to Walter Reed, I found myself at one time treating President Eisenhower's widow, former First Lady Mamie Eisenhower, following her (ultimately fatal) stroke.

GROWING UP IN CHICAGO

I was very fortunate that my growing up with a serious abnormality at birth was mediated by truly fabulous parents, Ralph and Kathryn Silverwood. By the last page, you may see that this book is not really about me, it is about them, If my story is at all inspiring, the credit is theirs.

Kathryn Silverwood

My mother was born to Clarence Moore and Clara Jane Moore, of Chicago. Clarence was Credit Manager and later Vice President of Charles A. Stevens, a well respected Chicago ladies' clothing store. At 17, My mother was sent to an exclusive finishing school–Lasell Seminary for Select Young Ladies, in Auburndale, Massachusetts. After two years at Lasell, she returned to her family in Chicago, and enrolled at the University of Chicago, in dietetics, later changing to sociology. It was here that she met my father.

Ralph J. Silverwood

My father, Ralph J. Silverwood, was born in Green Bay, Wisconsin, to Thomas P. Silverwood, an attorney, and Elizabeth (Lizzie) Will Silverwood. My mother's memoir tells me that "Lizzie was a wonderful and very modern woman. As a member of the Green Bay school board, she uncovered some corruption in the affairs of the school board president. When she revealed this, it led to an investigation whereby he was ousted. Then she became president, and she abolished the old rule that, when a teacher married, she automatically lost her job [in favor of a male 'breadwinner']."

My mother's memoir continues: "She [my father's mother] graduated from Carrol College, in Wisconsin, and taught school until she married. She ... had a sense of humor, and I'll never forget her advice when she visited us [as] newlyweds, 'Tata, if your husband wants you to go out with him, drop everything and go. The dirty dishes will wait for you. The housekeeping chores can be done later.' I thought, *Boy that from my mother-in-law!* I relished that advice." [10]

In 1896, when my father's father, Thomas P. Silverwood, finished law school at the University of Wisconsin in Madison, he rode his bicycle to Green Bay, about 135 miles, to seek engagement there as an attorney. That first Fall in Green Bay, he became acquainted with a "town team" of football players, then known as The Bays—initially organized in 1895 by one Fred Hulbert. In 1896 Tom Silverwood began playing with The Bays and soon became their captain and manager. In 1897, one player, Tom Skenandore, from the nearby Oneida Indian reservation, was paid twenty dollars per game (when the team had the money) and thus the team became "semi-professional." The other players "volunteered their injuries." It was said that, "Under Hulbert, Silverwood and Ed Krippner, the team advanced from a crew of street brawlers to a crack unit with a statewide reputation."[11] They were undefeated (4-0-1) in 1897; since there was then no league or sports commission, there was no one with more authority than themselves to declare them 1897 regional champions, and this they did.

[10] Kathryn Moore Silverwood, *As I Recall,* self-published memoir, p. 28.
[11] *Before They Were the Packers*, p. 24. Ed Krippner, a West Side tailor, was business manager for the team in the championship year of 1897.

The team subsequently attracted the sponsorship of Fred Hulbert's employer, a local canning company, and began wearing jerseys emblazoned with the name "Acme Packers." More than two decades later, when the National Football League (NFL) was

The Green Bay "town team," The Bays, were 1897 regional champions. My grandfather, T.P. Silverwood, is in the center, holding the ball.

organized in 1921, the former "town team" once known as The Bays, or the Green Bay City Team, was the third team to join up.

Though the modern Green Bay Packers are often reputed to have been the creation of Curly

Lambeau—who made a fully professional team of them and got them into the nascent NFL—Curly's celebrated association with the team has never superseded my family's regard for our ancestor T.P. Silverwood's role in the team's early development and success.[12] The modern Packers management has recognized T.P. Silverwood's early role in the founding of the team by posting his picture in their Hall of Fame at Lambeau Field.

In a unique ownership arrangement, the Packers became the possession of various and numerous Green Bay citizens, each of whom was permitted to own not more than 200 shares of stock in the corporation. Today, that form of ownership persists: over 360,000 of Green Bay's fans hold the Packers' widely distributed voting stock in the non-profit corporation. The Packers remain the only community-owned major-league professional sports team in the United States. Green Bay's nickname, "Titletown," honors their team's accomplishment in winning more NFL championships than any other—thirteen. The Chicago Bears are second with nine. [13]

I grew up rooting for and watching the Green Bay Packers on TV, with my father. Even today, after 50 years in Washington, D.C., I remain loyal to the Packers. Most Sundays, starting with pre-season games in August, I can be found watching the Washington Redskins play. But when they play the Packers, there is no divided loyalty. I'm a Packers fan, through and through, by birthright. Imagine my pride when, on December 3rd, 2015, Packers quarterback Aaron

---

[12] *Before They Were The Packers*, p. 24-32.
[13] Wikipedia, retrieved September 20, 2014.

Rodgers–with game time expired–having been allowed another play by a facemask penalty, threw the most amazing 70-yard, hail-Mary, jump-ball touchdown in football history, to win 27-20, capping the comeback from a 20-0 third-quarter deficit. I could not have been more thrilled, had T. P. Silverwood been reincarnated to make the throw himself.

HOW I BECAME....

When I was five, I started Kindergarten at Horace Mann Elementary School.[14] Because of my incontinence problem, Mrs. Fullwrath, my kindergarten teacher, had forethought to suggest to my parents that regular school might not always work for me as I progressed to higher grades. She told my parents about the Samuel Gompers School for handicapped children.[15] So when I turned six the next September, my parents enrolled me in the first grade at Samuel Gompers.

When my parents and I went to visit the Gompers school for the first time, we happened to see a handicapped child who, in passing by us in the hallway, happened to drop a paper he was carrying. When my father started to rush over to pick up the paper for the boy, the principal, Miss Courtney, abruptly stopped him. "We never do for the children what they can do for themselves," she said. "It's important to teach them that they *can* do for themselves, *not* that they *cannot* do for themselves."

Her philosophy was immediately vindicated and illustrated when, after substantial effort, the boy succeeded in retrieving his paper by himself–and looked up at Miss Courtney, beaming with pride in having demonstrated his sufficiency.

Recently, I heard on one of my favorite TV programs another version of this point of view. Doctor Phil McGraw said, on his TV program *Dr. Phil*, "One

---

[14] 8050 South Chappel Ave, Chicago, IL.
[15] 12302 W. 123rd St, Chicago, IL.

of the greatest injustices, one of the greatest insults that you can do to any child or adult that has any type of disability is to not require them to do and be all that they can do and be."[16]

Actually, Gompers wasn't just for *handicapped* children; the handicap school was just on the first floor. The "normal" children occupied the upper floors. In both cases, the school ran from kindergarten through the eighth grade. Most of the kids I went to school with on the first floor were much more physically handicapped than I. Though *mentally normal*, they all had serious *physical* problems–such as cerebral palsy, hemophilia, or crippling from polio. I had no such problem.

What's so interesting about Gompers is that, because I was there, and because I was a part of it, my classmates' handicaps weren't an issue for me. And my so-called handicap turned out not to be an issue for them either. Nobody there talked about it. Nobody asked about it or commented about it. There was never anything like that. Nobody expressed any curiosity about anyone else's handicap. There was no interest in that. At Gompers, being handicapped in some way, or in *any* way, was the "normal." We seemed to be more concerned with what the others *were* than with what they *weren't*. Because of that, we got to know the person. I think that was wonderful. To me that was the best part about being at Gompers.

By the time I was in first grade, I could walk well enough, albeit with a slight hitch, and I *wasn't* mentally handicapped. I did have what is called a "lazy eye." Although my individual eyes were

---

[16] Dr. Phil McGraw (TV Show), Season 8, Episode 178.

physiologically normal, my brain apparently didn't handle the signals from both eyes equally. In effect, with both eyes open, I was seeing with one eye only. This affected my peripheral vision on one side and kept me from perceiving depth (the relative distance of different objects from me). In second grade it was also discovered that I had some difficulty with reading. Even today I believe I have a slight learning disability for reading–a mild form of dyslexia–though never diagnosed.

Math was never my strong suit either, but I seemed to be bright enough and mobile enough that, before long, I found that I could be of help both to my fellow students and to the teachers

Why I Became A Speech Therapist

In the first or second grade, I became acutely aware that some of the kids were being excused, regularly, from one or another segment of the school day. These were the kids who had problems with speech, arising from motor-neural deficits of several varieties. These kids, singly or in groups, would leave the classroom to meet with the speech therapist. One time, I asked one of these kids what they did in "speech therapy." The answer was, "We play games!"

WELL! I thought. *They play games?* I was totally shocked! I was *really* angry! *Are you kidding me? They play games?! I want to play games, too!* I was incensed! I desperately wished that I could go and join the fun that was going on in the speech therapist's office! *How come I can't go and play games?*

And get out of geography!

Also, around this same time, I was becoming aware that some of the same kids–however bright they may have been inside; however much they may have been understanding exactly what was going on in class– had what I later learned to call *motor-speech* problems. For instance, I remember one girl, Mina Jackson, who had severe cerebral palsy. She seemed to understand everything, but she couldn't speak a word because of her severe motor impairment. So I would help her. I would stay in at recess and lunchtime to "talk" with her. I would put up on the chalkboard every letter of the alphabet; then I would point sequentially to each one– "a, b, c," and so on. She would indicate to me what letter would start her word, by showing a sort of generalized excitement–her whole body would start moving, rocking, and her eyes would get wider–and I would write that letter on the board. Then, for the second letter, we would start again with "a"–and on, and on. When we finally got written down a complete thought, she would practically jump up and down (or try to). When I enabled her in this way to actually "say" something that another could understand, it was just like letting her out of prison! You should have seen the expression of *joy* on her face! Like it was Christmas morning!

So, after all that work, what WAS it that Mina wanted so badly to say, that first time? In truth, that first expression, her first statement, is now lost to time; I don't remember it. Probably, though, it was just the expression of some basic need of the moment–maybe a need that she had experienced over and over and over again, without ever being able to say it. Probably something like, *"I need a drink of water."* [17]

Today, in professional speech therapy—65 years later—the chalkboard technique I used is embodied in an improved physical device that is called an "augmentative alternative communication (AAC) board." Actually, there are now several augmentative communications technologies, but they didn't have any of that when I was at Gompers.

By one means or another, I learned to understand, better than the teachers, what those of my classmates with severe speech problems were trying to say. For example, unlike Mina Jackson, Judy Dondelinger's speech was almost normal, and because I spent lots of time interacting with Judy—on the bus for an hour each way, at lunch and at recess—I could understand her very well. The teacher frequently would say, "Pam, what is Judy saying?" and I would interpret for her. That feeling of letting these other kids, my friends, out of communications prison had a powerfully engaging effect on me. In addition, of course, I had learned that if you were in speech therapy you were

---

[17] If that *was* Mina's first expression of need, I cannot help but draw a certain parallel with the beginnings of language for Helen Keller. As portrayed in the film, *The Miracle Worker*, Helen Keller's first word, coaxed out of her by her teacher, Anne Sullivan, was *"water."* Of course, Helen Keller was not just mute, but also *deaf* and *blind.* In contrast, Mina Jackson could *hear and see* perfectly well, evidently since birth. So, by school age, Mina had already learned a vocabulary—an association between the physical experience of objects (such as water) and the symbols used to represent objects: *words* (in her case, words both *heard* and *seen*). It simply remained for Mina to discover or be taught a technology for *expressing* her words in a way that another could perceive and understand.

NOT in geography! So, by the fourth grade, I had decided: *I will be a speech therapist when I grow up!*

People sometimes think of a handicap—theirs or another's—as a *road block* to becoming fully realized as an individual. But in my case, I think my handicap turned out in the end to be my *road map*. Were it not for my handicap, I might never have found my calling as a speech pathologist. It's true! As it happened, it was my years at Gompers, a school for the handicapped, that led me to know what my full realization as a helping professional—and a self-reliant adult person—could be. By fourth grade, I had decided: that is what I was going to do! I never changed my mind. There is no question of this: I would never have become a speech pathologist had I not had Spina Bifida—because I would never have *heard* of speech pathology, not until years later anyway.

At Gompers, I began to say to myself: *Hello! If I become a speech therapist*—the speech *pathologist* term came much later—*I can make a living, playing games! To heck with geography!* And the look on Mina Jackson's face, when I could say back to her, "Your shoulder hurts!" ("Oh! Thank goodness; someone *understands!*") Thus, the manner in which I *became* an independent and financially responsible adult was not *in spite of* my handicap and my years at Gompers, but *because of* those very circumstances.

At Gompers school for the handicapped, there was no laughing at other kids' misfortunes; it was a school that evidently taught that kind of sensitivity—to the "normal" kids! They really got it. They never made fun of us. They were remarkably kind! Even the "normal" kids in the *lowest grades* accepted us.

23

Ordinarily, kids can be brutal. These were more sensitive than kids of that age normally are. That seems very unique. I can't help but wonder whether the teachers of the non-handicapped kids at Gompers, with explicit forethought, taught them to be amazingly gentle, accepting, and sensitive with us. In fact, there is no question in my mind about that! Why don't we, today, teach that in every school in the nation?

What I realize now is that the *normal* kids at Gompers got something very special and unique also.

But, among the *handicap* kids, we didn't *think* of each other as *handicapped*. We were just kids! We teased *each other* all the time, just like "normal" kids do, but never with specific reference to a kid's handicap.

My husband once asked me, "Do you think your eight years experience at Gompers colored your outlook in general toward people who are different?"

Yes, I think I learned to treat handicapped people as normal because I saw how easy it would be to discriminate against *me*. I became sensitized to that possibility early on. For that reason, I feel that I am much less prejudiced against people who are different from me—such as people who are born of another race or with homosexual attractions. I am compelled to fight such prejudice. Everyone has the right to become as much, to get as much and as far, as they can, without others putting a damper on them. I powerfully want to fight for the rights and success of others because I remember so well the people who fought for me.

I saw real racial discrimination one summer, when my parents took our family on a car trip through the South. We came once to a service station in Alabama, where the restrooms were clearly marked: "Men," "Women," and "Colored." I couldn't believe it! I felt such anger! I thought, "Well, that's not right; we'll see about that!" I went toward the Colored door. Suddenly, one of the service station men came running after me, yelling out to me, urgently, "You can't go in there!" He physically prevented me, by standing in my path, from opening that door. Besides noticing me, he may have seen our license plate and thought, "I've got to teach these Yankees what's what down here!" I wanted so desperately to say, "But I'm colored!" Well, of course I couldn't carry it off, and thus I failed to end segregation in the South!

When my family vacationed at Corey Lake in Michigan, we ran into anti-semitism. Sometimes people think my family is Jewish because of our name– Silverwood. That name seems to say "Jewish" to some people. When my mother first phoned to make a reservation for our family vacation, she was told, "We don't rent to Jewish people." She just said, "We're not Jewish." That seemed to be enough, because she next heard, "Oh ... well ... that will be all right then."

Naturally, when I heard this, I resolved to integrate the Shore Acres Cottages by bringing along to the lake my Jewish friend, Frannie Levine. I don't know whether they ever wondered whether Frannie was Jewish, but we got away with it!

Harwa Kids' Club

Our family once visited Chicago's Field Museum, where we kids became fascinated with the mummy of the ancient Egyptian official Harwa.[18] Harwa was displayed wrapped up in linen and confined to a coffin-like box—I think now it is called a sarcophagus. But the display included an x-ray machine, which permitted us, when we pushed a button to activate an x-ray beam, to see the ancient Egyptian's skeleton. My brother Tom thought this was way cool, and he soon composed a ditty that went like this:

"Harwa, Harwa

X-Ray Harwa!"

A small boy nearby, observing six siblings and cousins bowing down before the mummy and hearing us chant this ditty, said "Mommy, what are they doing?"

"I don't know dear, but let's get out of here!" She seemed, somehow, on the verge of panic. It made her *very* nervous.

Well, after that museum visit, we never forgot the mummy Harwa. We formed a Harwa "admiration" society—a Harwa Club—and gave ourselves Harwa Club member numbers, in the order of our births. Cousin Ann was Harwa One; my brother Tom was Harwa Two; cousin Judy was Harwa Three. I was Harwa Four. Cousin Robbie was Harwa Five. My younger brother Jim was Harwa Six. For years afterward, whenever we all got together in Green Bay with our families for Thanksgiving or Christmas, we would call to order the latest meeting of the Harwa Club and conduct such business as our young imaginations could conceive. Also, over the years as it occurred to us, we initiated

[18] http://www.youtube.com/watch?v=ZDz10wKx0I0   Retrieved October 8, 2014.

my cousins (on my mother's side) Betty and Sara, and much, much, later, my husband David (Harwa Seven).

Jim's Broken Neck

When my younger brother Jim was around 3 to 5 years old, we had a fence in our yard that separated our back yard from the alley in the rear. I came out of the house one day and heard Jim crying. "Fence fell on me," he sobbed. "My neck hurts."

The evening was spent trying to comfort Jim—heating pad, aspirin, etc. Next morning though, Jim was taken to the hospital, and it was found that he had broken a couple of vertebrae in his neck. He wound up wearing a cast on his upper body that went clear up to surround his neck. He wore this for several weeks.

After some time, he got itchy inside the cast and he couldn't scratch it. So, we learned to stick a table knife under the cast to scratch his itch.

He had said that the fence "fell on me." But I often wonder whether he was actually climbing on the fence, when his weight broke it, and the fence fell down with *and on* him!

Summer Fun

We had a lot of fun in the summertime, when school was out. We drank a lot of cherry Cokes and ate a lot of rainbow sherbet cones. Before my parents joined the Beverly Hills Country Club, my mom would take us swimming at the beach on Lake Michigan. Lake Michigan was very cold, so when we began to swim at the Country Club instead, it was well appreciated.

Duke Zeibert's

Duke Zeibert's was a famous and fancy restaurant in Washington D.C. I was there on a vacation trip with my father and mother, my uncle Bunk, cousin Betty Moore, and my brother, Tom. Zeibert's had great food, and some of the best pickles I had ever tasted. I wanted to take some of those delicious pickles home with me, but I was too inhibited to ask. In those days, it was not nearly as routine as now, to take food home after the end of a restaurant meal. People were afraid of seeming "cheap," I guess. The pose was always, "I'd like to take this home for my dog," or, more succinctly, "May I have a doggie bag, please?"

Before making any such conventional request, as we discussed the issue around the table, my Uncle Bunk turned to me and said, "Pam, just tell them you have a dog that's crazy about pickles!"

We got the pickles, and we've been laughing about it ever since.

Dog Doings

My father was the outgoing President of the Chicago Real Estate Board. He was going to go downtown one evening to the Conrad Hilton Hotel for an event at which he was going to be given some award and give a speech. It was morning, and he was in the bathroom.

Suddenly, we heard some excited language. My father sounded like he was close to having a heart attack!

"The dog; he's got my *teeth*!" he shouted. It was just a partial plate, but it was several front teeth–the teeth that would show the most when he smiled. Or talked! Or gave a speech!

So the whole family joined in, running and chasing the dog, Charlie, all around the house. Dad was excitedly chasing Charlie—and at the same time yelling at us not to "scare the dog." The more we chased, the more Charlie enjoyed the game.

Finally, we cornered Charlie and my father recovered his teeth. After a thorough washing of the teeth, all was well.

After Charlie, our next dog was one that Tom found as a stray in the woods. Tom named him Eilrahc, which is "Charlie" spelled backwards!

One of my favorite dogs was Peggy. One thing about Peggy was that she always wanted to sleep with me. So I always wanted to get to bed before Peggy knew I was going, because she wanted to sleep in my bed!

Peggy was a large Dalmatian, and she would sleep on a diagonal. So, once she was in my bed, there was no room for me!

If she got there first, I was dead meat!

Eventually, I would have to just push her off—but I always felt terrible, doing it.

What I would do was this: when it was time to go to bed, I would steal toward the stairs as quietly as I could, but she'd always know I was doing it. Every time, when I got three-quarters of the way up the stairs, here came Peggy, flying past me and into the bedroom and onto the bed, sprawled from one corner to its opposite!

My good friend, Sue Sweet, said that we had to take our dogs to obedience training. So she and I joined a class for obedience training, with our respective dogs.

Sue's dog was really obedient. Sue was just a master at getting Muggs to heel, to stay, and all the things that you have to do in obedience training. Peggy was never as manageable as Muggs. I knew that Muggs was going to win the prize, the last day of class, for the most obedient dog. Sue had done so much more training than I. But on the night of the final exam, my dog, Peggy, did unusually well, and we won the prize! I was mortified; I felt very bad for Sue, who really deserved the prize. And, crazy as it may seem, I *still* think Peggy won because of *the way I walk.*

A month later, Peggy got out of the house. I went outside to call her back. I called and called, but she didn't come. Finally, I went back into the house. Five minutes later, a man came to the door and told us, "I'm sorry, but I've hit your dog." Peggy had run out in front of the man's car, and it was all over. Peggy was killed, and the whole family grieved for *the obedience-winning dog*, who hadn't come when called, at the cost of her life. She was five or six years old, at the prime of her life when it happened.

Nancy Blair–The Don K Ranch

Across the street, there was a girl almost my same age–Nancy Blair. Nancy and I became the best of friends, and we remain so to this day. Nancy's family went, every summer, to a dude ranch in Colorado called The Don K Ranch. They would come home at the end of their vacation with wonderful stories of ranch life. Much Later, I went there one summer with my husband David and son Andrew. We went for trail rides twice a day, often carrying a picnic lunch with us, and at night there were barn dances with folk and square dancing. One day, near the end of the week, we participated in a "rodeo" in the Ranch's own arena. It was a wonderful week that I'll remember forever. Andrew had a wonderful time, and we used a picture of him with "his" horse in our Christmas letter.

After our week at the Don K, we attended the Colorado State Fair, at Pueblo, Colorado, where we witnessed a real rodeo from the grandstand.

A few months after our visit, we received a letter from the Don K announcing that the previous summer had been the last year the Don K would be operated as a dude ranch. The Don K had been sold to a party that wanted it as a private family ranch. After years and years of hoping that I would someday see and experience the Don K for myself—if we had not gone that year, the possibility would have been lost forever. I will always be thankful that we got to visit the Don K when we did.

I never got to the Don K Ranch as a child. This party photo shows the closest I ever got to a Horse in those years.

PIVOTAL PEOPLE

You Were My Inspiration, Pam!

Because of my "handicap," my father had long thought that I would never be able to support myself. So, long after I was grown up and had moved away to take a great job, he confided, "You know, Pam, *you're* the reason for *my* success. I was really motivated," he said, "because I knew that I had to make enough money that you would be supported for life." He had done so well in real estate that, when he was not quite 65, he sold his real estate business (and the house I grew up in) and moved with my mother to Florida, into a nice three-bedroom bungalow at the 15th Tee of a great golf club.

I've already said that my dad was my hero, and I believe that he loved me in a very special way. I was, of course, his only daughter, so that helped.

But, no one ever treated me as if I were *smart*–and that included my father.

I remember my father getting into discussions sometimes with my two brothers. Whether the subject was baseball or philosophy (my father had been a philosophy major), I could never get into the conversation. Once, the subject was music. My parents were fans of classical music and the opera, an enthusiasm that my older brother, Tom, came very much to share. On this occasion, the "men" were talking about what made for "good" music compared to lesser music. I suppose my father may have been drawing on his college studies in philosophy, including the philosophy of aesthetics. Whatever the trend of that particular discussion, I remember suggesting, from the fringe of the gathering, that perhaps good music could be a matter of personal taste. Instead of entertaining my thought as a worthy counterpoint, the three males immediately rejected my idea as completely unmeritorious, and they stuck fast to their collective, conventional wisdom, whatever it was.

My Summer In Real Estate

One summer while I was in high school, my father gave me a clerical job in his real estate office, Silverwood Realty. I was thrilled to have a summer job, let alone the chance to work with my father—riding all the way in the car, to and from work, every day!

I'm sure my parents thought—and maybe I feared too—that the only thing I might ever do job-wise would be something clerical.

I typed and filed, answered phones and took in rent money—everything a summer intern could be asked to do. And I kept my eyes and ears open, hoping to learn something about my father's business and the world in general. I certainly saw my father in many situations, and I watched carefully how he handled himself in them.

I noticed one thing repeatedly. A significant part of my father's business was managing residential rental properties, for himself as well as other owner-landlords. This occasioned situations in which a tenant became dissatisfied with some aspect of their apartment home or its equipment. Sometimes a tenant would come into the office to complain, really upset and angry about a situation. Dad would invite the person into his inner office and securely close the door. Ten or twenty or thirty minutes later they would come out, and invariably everything had changed. The irate and/or loud complaints had disappeared, and the tenant and my father would come out practically arm in arm, laughing and joking like old friends. I never tired of seeing how effectively my father could disarm the most hostile client or customer. I think a major part of his technique was just to listen earnestly to the problem and how it was affecting the complainant. I have since tried to adapt my father's people skills to my own purposes and profession. As Oprah Winfrey has said, everyone wants at least three things in their relationships–personal or business. They want to know that they have been *seen*, been *heard*, and what they say *matters* to the person with whom they are interacting. Oprah did not reach the pinnacle of her renown until after my father retired to Florida and a life of bridge and golf. Nevertheless, I think his business relationships and philosophy closely resembled the values that Oprah often promoted.

My father was a very formal, dignified man. He would don a coat and tie, just to walk to the corner and mail a letter. But he once ran out of a hotel room *in his underwear*, to help rescue a drowning man from the surf. As he struggled to shore with his burden–seeing onlookers standing agape, as if paralyzed–he called out, "For God's sake–*give us a hand!*"[19]

---

[19]My brother Tom was older than I, so his memory of this event is more replete with detail. This is the whole story, as Tom remembers it:

"I was thinking about Dad in Ft. Lauderdale wearing only boxers. You only told half the story. Here's mine; use it if you wish.

"In spring, 1956, I spent the morning swimming in some pretty heavy surf, body surfing, diving into waves and having a good time, in Fort Lauderdale, FL, which one can do at age 20 or so. No way, Jose, at my present age of 80. Satisfied that I'd conquered the current, I retired to the cottage and poured myself a scotch: that one can also do at age 80. Casually, I peered out the window and saw a man frantically waving his arms. Curious, I sauntered out to the porch and heard him screaming for help.

"The gent was about 1/4 of a mile south of our cottage, but when I observed a young fellow diving in to assist, I thought, "This guy will need some help." I gently placed the scotch on a nearby umbrella table, dove back into the surf and swam out to the man and the young blond fellow, whom Pam would probably describe as "a hunk." When I arrived, the man gave up and went unconscious, and Hunk and I each took an elbow to hold him out of the water. We started to bring this dead weight in, when fortunately, a third man arrived with a navy blue air mattress over which we could drape our victim.

"I turned to my right and gasped as my father, clad only in white boxer shorts, had swum out to help us. 'What the (bleep) are you doing out here, old man? ' I queried, aghast that my 53 year old venerable father would dare join the party. When one is 20, 53 is the epitome of geezerdom. Dad just smiled and put his shoulder against the mattress.

"All went well, until we hit the surf near the shore. There Hunk and I held on to the victim for dear life as the surf rolled all of us hard against the stones and sand. When we arose from the waters, the victim's weight trebled, and we asked the crowd gathered on the beach if any might give us aid. A big murmur of assent ensued as the audience woke up, 'Oh, yes. Of course!' Then several folk helped us get the gent down on the beach. By this time my mother had gamboled down from the cottage only to see her husband standing there, unclad but for the boxers. As gently as she could, she intoned, 'Ralph, don't you think you ought to go back and put some clothes on?' To which Dad uttered, 'Oh, yes. OK, I'm going, Tot.'

"In the crowd was a girl named "Judy Jones," with whom I had attended Morgan Park High School two years earlier. "Judy" was an extremely religious, Bible thumping, do-gooder type who now attended Wheaton College in west suburban Chicago. Since "Judy" seldom, if ever, thought herself mistaken about anything, she had the propensity to take over situations at will. Here, she began to assert herself, but Hunk's father intervened by informing

So, never let it be said that my father was always in business garb. Once, in Ft. Lauderdale on vacation, he went informal!

My father had a ton of pithy sayings or capsule philosophies that he used to instruct or smilingly chide me. For example, if I enthused over some item I saw advertised *and discounted* at retail—exclaiming over how much money I could "save" by buying it, he might say, with a twinkle, "Gosh, Pam—you're losing money every minute you're not buying one!" Alternatively, on some other occasion, he might say, "If you don't need it, it's not a bargain." One of my father's sayings that I used myself, when I became a mother, was "Being a parent is not a popularity contest."

He became president of the Chicago Real Estate Board, and later, president of the Illinois Association of Realtors. He retired as president of the Association at a banquet held at the Conrad Hilton Hotel, at which the guest speaker was Defense Secretary Charles E. Wilson. U.S. Senator Everett Dirksen of Illinois was there also. (This was the occasion just before which the dog stole Dad's teeth.) My father interacted very easily with such political and economic leaders.

"You Can Do It, Pam!"

As I neared the completion of the eighth grade, I expected to be transferred to a handicap high school

---

her that he was a doctor and could take over now. Which he then did.

"The 'victim' turned out to be a lawyer from Kentucky (I think, Lexington). He invited Hunk (I can't remember his real name) and me over to his place for drinks and many thank yous. I do remember that Hunk had a younger sister, with whom Pam became pretty good friends."

program, at some new school–Spaulding High School–that I knew little about. One day, Nancy Blair said to me: "Pam, why don't you go to Morgan Park High School like all the other kids we know. You don't need to go to a handicap school any more!"

"You think so? You really think I can?" I said.

"Of course you can. How are you handicapped anyway?" she said. "You walk a little funny. What else? You don't seem handicapped to me at all. You can do it, Pam!"

Nancy didn't know about my urinary incontinence. I kept it even from her!

I talked to my mother about it–regular high school, that is. She was very non-committal.

"Well, I don't know, she said. Let's think about it.... I will talk to your father about it.... We will see."

I know my parents were very nervous about me trying to go to a "normal" high school. After all, they had been told I would never walk, never talk, and would be mentally handicapped. I was surely walking and talking, but they had little to go on in assessing my capacity for a "normal" education. They never gave any indication that they thought I was "smart" in any way. After all, I had been in a handicap school for nearly eight years. I had done all right, they guessed, but who had I been competing with? Not much competition, they probably thought.

More important, there was also the incontinence. Gompers was accustomed to handling the special needs of kids who were not completely normal. There would be no such accommodations in "normal" high school, we knew. What would happen if (*when*) I had an "accident?" they must have thought. They didn't know how smart handicapped kids could be!

Well, they decided to let me try it. If I had an accident at school, I was just to call home, and my mother would come and get me and take me home so I could change clothes. Once again, as always, Mom would step in and help me present myself as just as normal as possible. She was amazing! Mom was always there for me. I wasn't going to "fail," if she could help it! She never held me back, never got in my way! She never said, "You can't do that," or "You shouldn't do that." She had such a good balance; she was there when I needed her, then she stepped back to let me be me, even to fail, if that was what happened.

Now that contradicts what I just said, that she wasn't going to let me fail, if she could help it. I can't resolve the conflict. I just know she was the best mother on the planet. She was amazing!

Even when she must have been terrified for me! She gave me my *freedom*! It was an amazing balance she had there—as a mother! And my Dad was just as good.

And I didn't fail. I eventually graduated from Morgan Park High School, on schedule, with all of my age peers. Well, I did graduate with the *January* class—a result of my absence in my junior year, for kidney surgery.

"How Did You Do At The Dentist?"

In high school, I took the train to and from school. Every day, I would walk from the train to the school, a couple of blocks. One day, Judy Brooks, a fellow train rider, asked me, "What are you doing this weekend, Pam?"

"I have to go to the dentist tomorrow," I said. I really hated the dentist. I absolutely dreaded the needle being stuck into my gums, to numb me for the drilling, drilling, drilling, with those buzzing, buzzing old-fashioned mechanical drills. Sometimes, I thought I would faint. I suppose I told my casual acquaintance about my fear and antipathy.

Monday morning, Judy inquired of me again: "How did it go at the dentist, Pam?"

Well, however it went at the dentist on that occasion, the thing I remember, the thing I have never forgotten over all the years, is how good it felt to have her ask me about it again—after her weekend of thinking about and doing whatever happens in the life of an extremely popular girl, for she was extremely popular.

The more I thought about Judy remembering anything at all about me, after her date (as I supposed) with some really cute guy at some very current new movie—I began to wonder: Do you suppose that's why she's so popular? Does she ask those personal questions of everyone, the way she did with me?

It sure made me feel good when she did it. I found myself thinking that maybe I would like to be her friend. Is that what all those other people who like her think and feel about her? I resolved, then and there, to try to be like her. And I continued to try to be like her—all the time, through the rest of high school, through college, graduate school, in my teaching—in all of my personal and professional contacts.

David now tells me that I am a "friend-magnet," that I have charisma. That means, he says, that people want to follow me or really want to be my friend. Well, if that's true, I owe it all to that one pair of conversations with Judy Brooks about the dentist!

By the way, it's David who says that I have charisma. *I never said that!*

I once heard Dr. Phil ask, on his TV program, "Who are your pivotal people? Who are the seven people who most caused turning points in the course of your life." I realized then that <u>Nancy Blair</u>, who believed (and argued) that I could successfully transfer to a "normal" high school–and <u>Judy Brooks</u>, who had remembered over a weekend my rendezvous with the dentist–had been two of my pivotal people.

Others were:

- My father, who said, "She's coming home with us," when I was born.
- In graduate school, Dr. Van Riper–who held the straws as I drew the lucky one, the one that sent me to the Hines Veterans Administration (VA) Hospital, outside of Chicago, where I learned about aphasia and chose that as my career path. This eventually brought me to Walter Reed.
- Joanne Schwartz, the "Fairy Godmother" who dragged me to the event where I met my husband, David.

In addition there were these two pivotal *events*, that made all the difference in my later life:

- David and I spent a day together taking care of my nephew, 18-month-old John Douglas

Silverwood–which prompted David to raise again the subject of adoption.

- A *Business Week* article showed David (and thus me) how we could find an infant to adopt–in spite of our ages–which at that time was about 46.

It's very curious, maybe just a convenient coincidence, that the seven *people/events* named above are the same in number as the *pivotal people* that Dr. Phil says the average person has!

MORGAN PARK

Sororities

Once I was enrolled in Morgan Park High School—my nearby "normal" high school—I began hearing about sororities. The sororities met in people's homes, off campus, but were comprised of students from the high school. Early in the fall, I was invited to a party given by one of the three sororities. I didn't even *know* the person who invited me, but I thought: *A party! Who wouldn't want to go to a party?* I didn't know much about the sororities either until I got invited to the party—a "rush party"—and even then I didn't realize that what I was going to *was* a rush party. I didn't know what a rush party was, what it was *for*.

My mother must not have known there were sororities in high school, either (though she surely knew about them in college). Mom probably thought they were just some kind of social club. Maybe she thought that the high school kids were just aping the Greek letter names of college sororities. But in fact, they were aping the whole thing, and I was on my own, as far as understanding what it was all about.

Before I knew it, I was invited to *three* parties, each to be put on by one or another of the three sororities comprised of students from Morgan Park High School. Wow, what fun! I had no concept that these "rush" parties had something to do with recruiting new members—something to do with looking over the new girls to see who might be a good fit as a new member for this or that sorority. Nobody told me about that.

The night of the first party, I arrived and saw some girls working in the kitchen, doing something to prepare food and serve it for the party. I walked right into the kitchen and said, "Can I help? What can I do to help?" I just pitched right in, as I would do at any get-together.

I would have been a wreck, trying to fit in, if I'd known what a rush party was, what the stakes were. But I was totally relaxed. Hey, I *liked* parties!

After attending the rush parties of all three sororities, I was invited to *join* all three! *Hey, I just went to have a good time! And now they want me to join up!* Every one of those sororities wanted me to join them. *What do you know?*

I might have *joined* all three, but someone told me I had to choose just one! I couldn't even remember who was at any of the parties, or who was a member of what. For me, they all just blended into the same whirl. Well, after I found out that you were supposed to join only one, I didn't know what to do. D.U.C. had been the first to ask me, and it seemed fair to join the first one that asked. What's more, D.U.C was considered somehow the "top" sorority—whatever that meant. It seemed like the handwriting was on the wall. So I joined D.U.C., and there I was, a sorority girl!

Each sorority had a different way of initiation. Part of the D.U.C initiation was this: if you happened to come across any D.U.C *member*, you had to curtsey and say, "How do you do, my lady." Also, for my initiation, I lip-synched to Patti Page's recording of *How Much Is That Doggie In The Window*; that was my "talent!"

Very soon, though, I found that sorority life was not to my liking

I had many friends who weren't invited to party with or join any sorority. They would ask, "Why wasn't I invited?" I didn't have a clue why I had been asked, let alone why they were not. *Maybe they were not asking the right people about their dental appointments!*

The very next semester, we had another "rush" party and I soon found myself in a meeting—a sort of "after action" conference to decide which of the new girls, who'd attended the latest party, were worthy of becoming one of us.

At the meeting, I began to hear other members say things like, "She doesn't have enough cashmere sweaters!" "She's never going to be popular!" "I don't think she's a D.U.C. girl; I'm going to vote no on her!"

There I was, thinking, *I don't have ANY cashmere sweaters! What am I doing here?*

Oh boy! What a shock! It was disgusting. The more they talked, the more I thought about it. The more I thought about it, the more I began to realize that few of my friends had been invited to our party. (Maybe *I* should have invited them, but I was still very new to all this.) Of those girls who *were* invited to the party, my "sisters" were not going to let them in as members, unless they met some mysterious criteria for our exclusive society of "the best girls!" Before the meeting was even over, I said silently to myself, *I'm not coming back to* this!

So I went inactive in "my" sorority, never to return. I just stopped going, and I never regretted it. And, when it came time to select a college to attend after high school, I carefully and deliberately—after pointed research—chose a college that did not have any sororities. (It does now; but it didn't have them then!)

ILLINOIS STATE

After high school, I moved on to college at the Illinois State Normal University in Normal, Illinois,[20] chosen of course because it had a speech and language program and NO sororities.

Did my need to "fit in" determine my decision to join a sorority in high school? I don't know, but I do believe that a need to fit in explains why I started *smoking* in college. (I never smoked at home. My parents never knew! My mother lived to be 103, and I'm sure that I never told her.)

When I worked at Walter Reed Hospital with men who had lost their larynxes–their voices–to cancer, I saw one man smoking by putting the cigarette to the hole in his neck that was left as a result of surgically losing his larynx. (The larynx that *had to be* removed, because of smoking-induced *cancer!*) I realized then, the vicious trap involved in smoking! I saw the light, and I *stopped smoking.* It was not easy; it was very, very hard. But I'm terribly glad I finally stopped.

Years later–after I *stopped* smoking, I came better to understand my motive for beginning. Because of the atrophied muscles in my legs and the weakness of my ankles, I couldn't wear high heels. So that symbol of grown-up-ness and sophistication was unavailable to

---

[20] Current name, Illinois State University. I like to say that they took out the word "Normal" after I got there! The town was (re)named Normal in February 1865 and officially incorporated on February 25, 1867. The name was taken from the Illinois State Normal University, a normal school (teacher-training institution) located there. The school was renamed Illinois State University after becoming a general four-year university. –Wikipedia, retrieved November 14, 2015.

me. I am sure that I started smoking in an attempt to seem more mature and sophisticated, in part because I couldn't wear high heels.

No sooner was I on the college campus than I started to join into many activities, starting with secretary of the freshman class. Wasn't this what college was all about? But before long, I began to ask myself, "But when Do I Study?"

After a couple of months, I was called into the office of Dr. Harold Phelps, the head of Special Education, to discuss my scores on the entry exams that I had taken a few weeks earlier. "I don't know what you're doing here," he declared. "Your scores are all in the bottom quartile of college freshmen, nationally. This is a very challenging school. Statistics suggest that you will never graduate from here." Well, that made me mad, and I resolved that, somehow, I would prove him wrong.[21]

At that time, I didn't know what was meant by the phrase, "study hard." I had no clue how you had to study, to be "studying hard." I *thought* I *was* studying hard. I wasn't!

It wasn't until my senior year that I had a roommate who *really* studied *hard*! She studied morning, afternoon, and night. *Wow*, I thought. So *that's* what they mean by "study hard." It was the best thing that could have happened to me. I watched her. I

---

[21] Harold Phelps, Ph.D., Head of the Department of Special Education, Illinois State University at Normal, Illinois. "You don't belong in college. Your entrance test scores are too low. You'll never graduate." Personal counseling, session, Fall semester, 1958.

copied her. And I *learned*; I mean, I learned how to *study*! Then, finally, I studied to *learn*!

One summer, when I was home from college, my mother was wanting to take golf lessons at the Beverly Hills Country Club, where my parents had become members. She thought I might like to take lessons too, so I want along. We went to what I remember as an informational meeting, conducted at the club, to tell about the teaching program.

There must have been about 20 women there, to find out about golf lessons from the golf "Pro." He said, "We will go around the room. Please tell us your name." As they were going around the room, my mother leaned over to me and whispered into my ear, "Just tell them your name is Pam Silverwood."

I am home from *college*, and my mother is *coaching* me how to respond to a request *to say my name?!!*

"Just tell them your name is Pam Silverwood," she said. We never let her forget it. Thereafter, whenever someone in the family began giving someone elaborate instructions in something exceedingly simple, someone in the family would remember to quip, "Just tell them your name is Pam Silverwood!"

In her defense: remember that this was the mother who had been told, "She'll never walk or talk, and she'll be mentally retarded." This was the mother who had changed my bed and laundered my sheets and pajamas, *every single day,* until I was nine years old–and never once complained.

This was the mother who stood ready, throughout my high school years, to drop everything and come to school to get me, should I have an "accident" at school. I can't say it enough–she was, without question, the best mother on the planet.

Once, as an adult, when I protested some evidence of my Mom's (over) protectiveness, she said to me, "Just remember, Dear, no matter how old you get, *you'll always be my little girl!*

Now that I am the mother of a "little boy"—who long-since stretched to six-feet-five and recently observed his 30th birthday—I do now understand, better than ever, my mother's words.

Summer School In Hawaii

One summer, I wanted to go to Hawaii, to attend summer classes there, and do some sunning and swimming.

"Sure you can!" said my mother. "Your grandmother left some money for your education. Since you're attending a state school, it's not costing so much; you can use that money for your summer session."

So, while my roommates in Hawaii took classes like underwater basket weaving, I took "Anthropology" and "Tests and Measurements." (I had to have a statistics class to graduate, and Tests and Measurements was the only statistics class I thought I had a prayer of passing.) So, while my friends could go to the beach every day after classes, I was stuck indoors studying one of the hardest classes I ever took in my life! But I passed. And I did get to spend about half the summer in Hawaii.

Some of my other classes caused me even more worry. For example, in my last semester, I had to take a class called "Speech Science." It was required for my major in Special Education with an emphasis on Speech Therapy. It was all about vibrations in the air and the vibrations they caused in the eardrum and the inner ear—as well as the physics of sound transmission through various materials. The grade in the class was determined by only two exams for the entire semester: the midterm and the final exam.

I failed the midterm; so, the only way I could pass the class and graduate was if I could "ace" the final. I never studied so hard in all my life. I really didn't understand the subject matter very much; the only thing I could do was to try to memorize the textbook from the front cover to the back. There was one other girl, Jane Nelson, who was in the same boat that I was in. After the exam, I was too scared to even go and see my grade, where it was posted outside the professor's office door. So, Jane went for both of us.

"Iron your gown; we made it!" she shouted, as she barged through the door to my room. I could graduate after all. It was a good thing. My parents had already made their plans to attend my graduation ceremony!

ORANGEVILLE AND PEARL CITY

I graduated with a double major, in elementary education and special education. Shortly before my graduation, the Superintendent of Schools for the Orangeville Schools, of Orangeville Illinois, came to Illinois State University (at Normal, Illinois) and found me. He made an appointment to interview me at my dormitory. Before long, I was hired as the Speech Therapist for *two* schools: Orangeville Elementary and Pearl City Elementary. Because I was to work in two schools, I was offered more money than any of my fellow education graduates, $5,200 for the 10-month year. That was 1962. By September my father had bought me a green Chevrolet Corvair automobile, and off I went to my first professional job.

Pearl City

Pearl City had never had a speech therapist before, so I started up the program there. I split the time between the two towns. Pearl City gave me an entire empty classroom for my office, and I set about ordering the supplies and equipment that I needed.

In November, 1963, we heard over the intercom that President John Kennedy had been shot, while riding in a motorcade in Dallas. I remember telling the kids who were with me that they should remember where they were when they heard that announcement, because this was a moment of history that they should remember forever.

I was tapped to direct the Junior Class play, *The Ghosts Go West.* I didn't know anything about directing a play; I had taken exactly zero classes in theatre or acting or directing. But it was clear to me that the

Superintendent of Pearl City Schools didn't understand much of what speech therapy was about; he must have thought, "Well, she's about speech, and what is a play but speech? Pam can do it! "

So, I directed the play. Every school night, I went back from my apartment in Freeport, to Pearl City Elementary, for rehearsals. After our performances, people said it was good—and my older brother Tom came with a friend from Glenn Ellyn, Illinois, to see it. I got lots of accolades; everybody said it was a great play. I don't know how I managed it, but I guess I just didn't know enough to be afraid.

Orangeville

We had a parents' night, and I was all dressed up in my best dress-up dress and pearls to meet parents. I was in my office at Orangeville. A mouse ran right behind me. Next moment the Superintendent walks in—and I am standing up on top of my desk. He laughed hysterically. I got down, because I was more afraid of the "Super" than I was of the mouse.

That, of course, was the Superintendent who had hired me out of Illinois State.

He called my little green Corvair my "rotten avocado" car.

I was well respected and well utilized there. I made some nice friends. It was a good job. I ate my lunch for 25 cents in the school cafeteria.

One winter I skidded off the road in the snow, on my way to school. The school bus came by, and all the kids pointed and waved and laughed from the windows. "Look, Miss Silverwood is stuck in the snow!"

53

Finally a farmer came with his tractor and pulled me out. I guess someone must have called the farmer and told him of my plight. No damage to the car or to me, but I was certainly late to school that day.

There were many truly nice, dedicated teachers. But I was pretty busy with my kids. Especially with starting up the program at Pearl City. I did a lot of lecturing, at PTA and staff meetings, about what speech therapy had to offer. I handled, almost exclusively, articulation problems: "eisch cream" for ice cream (lateral lisp); "eith cream" (frontal lisp); "wabbit" for rabbit, and so on.

There was a little first-grade girl, named Brenda, who came back in the fall, for second grade, and seemed to have completely regressed over the summer. We had worked very successfully in first grade, on her "W for R" ("wabbit" for rabbit) problem. Now, at the outset of the new fall term, I was re-screening all the kids in her second grade class. When I tested Brenda—to my shock and horror—she was talking just the way she had in first grade—before I treated her for a full year! I was astonished! Not to mention, shocked!

Immediately, I was seized by every insecurity I'd ever felt. I was almost hearing the words, "She'll never walk or talk, and she'll be mentally retarded." Here I was, in my second year of practice, sporting two bachelor's degrees—Elementary Education and Special Ed—and I had *failed*! I'm thinking to myself, *I'm not good at this! I can't do it! I'll have to go to the principal and admit that the job is too much for me, and then find some other line of work.*

54

Stop this, Pam! I said under my breath. *Don't jump to conclusions before you get all the facts. First, find out just what is going on with this child!*

I said, "Brenda! What has happened to you? At the end of last year, you were talking fine. What happened to you over the summer?"

Brenda began to pucker up, looking down at her lap, seeming just about to cry....

"I just wanted to come back to Speech Club!" she said plaintively, almost tearfully—and then, with *perfect articulation:* "We had *so* much fun last yea*R* (sniff)!"

I wanted to hug the dear child. I said, "Brenda, we can still be *friends!* Would you like to bring your lunch to my office today? You can always come to see me, and you will be my friend."

Thinking back now, I wish there had been an advanced speech club to which I could send Brenda. In a high school, there might have been a debating society or a theatre class for her. I feel sad still for Brenda's feelings of loss, her grieving for a joyous time, now constructively but melancholically come to an end.

I guess I had a way of making "Speech Club" a positive experience, of rewarding the kids for their effort and improvement. Years later, I created an activity to fix a certain speech problem with an hilarious exercise I called "Peanut Butter Sandwich." More on that in a later chapter.

I worked my tailbone off in those three years. Two schools was a big load; I began to understand why they had offered me more money, to start, than I ever expected. But I wanted to go back and get my Master's degree. I *still* wanted to work in a hospital.

NEW HORIZONS

When I was an undergraduate at Illinois State, Professor Phelps, the head of Special Education, told me that I was in the bottom quarter of my class, as measured by my entrance exams. He said that I'd never graduate. Mrs. Richardson, who was second in the administration of the Speech Pathology program, was also a part time academic adviser. She was a bit more indirect about it; she told me that I should begin to consider alternate life plans. She said, "You're going to want to get married and have kids." I thought–*Ha! Who's going to marry me? I probably can't even _have_ kids.*

When I went on to my Master's degree at Western Michigan University (1965), after working three years in the Illinois schools, the picture really turned around. The faculty at Western Michigan were extremely positive about me. Dr. Van Riper, the famous expert on stuttering, was my mentor. I was finally affirmed. It was a turning point in my life; as far as I know, there was never a negative word said about me at Western Michigan. The faculty treated me almost as an equal. They gave me the hardest patients. At Western Michigan, I felt like a star!

Decades later, in 2015, my classmate Barry Guitar revealed to me that Dr. Van Riper had said then of me that "Pam is one of the very few non-stutterer therapists who really understand stuttering." Dr. Van Riper was of course himself a stutterer.

Stuttering

I had chosen Western Michigan for my Masters Degree work, of course, because that was where the renowned stuttering expert, Dr. Van Riper, taught, and I had been drawn to the problem of stuttering as my biggest area of interest in Speech Pathology. As part of my clinical work in stuttering, I had a patient with a profound stutter on the consonant "H." Not only that, but he was from Australia. "How is that important," you might ask."

Well, being from Australia, he spoke with the English broad A ... which sounds like "Ah." So that, when he stuttered on the consonant "H," instead of "Ha-Ha, Ha-Ha, Ha-Ha, Happy Birthday," he would say, "Hah-Hah, Hah-Hah, Hah-Hah, Hahppy Birth-dye!"

After working in the clinic for some time with this patient, it was time to take him out into the public to practice overcoming his fear, to practice getting his message across to a stranger—often an unknowing and unsympathetic stranger—in spite of his propensity (amplified by anxiety) to stutter, and the stranger's likely impatience with him. We would go out onto the campus, or out onto a public sidewalk, and he would approach strangers, one by one, and practice, practice, practice.

The next step, was to turn the anxiety up a notch or two. On the telephone, the stakes are even greater for a stutterer. On the telephone, you cannot see the other person, so you cannot tell, from the other person's facial expression and body language, how you are coming across—or if they are still listening. Worse, the other person cannot *see* your silent struggle, so the potential for empathy is lost. Without the normal, continuous two-way feedback of face-to-face conversation, the fear of the stutterer is greater, his stuttering is worse, and the other person's impatience (even anger) may grow. Worse still, the listener may hang up on you.

For my Australian patient, since his problem sound was "H," I looked in the yellow pages under the H's, and I found a retail establishment named *Harry's Hardware Store*. I asked my client to telephone Harry's Hardware store, verify that in fact he had *reached* "Harry's Hardware Store," and inquire about the price of Hammers. It went something like this:

"Heh-Heh, Heh-Heh, Heh-Heh, Hello. Is this Hah-Hah, Hah-Hah, Hah-Hah, Hahry's Hah-Hah, Hah-Hah, Hah-Hah, Hah-Hah, Hah-Hah, Hah-Hah, Hardware Store?

At this point, I would hear a pause, then:

"What is the price of your Hah-Hah, Hah-Hah, Hah-Hah, Hahmmers?"

By this time, I could no longer contain it; I started to crack up! Watching his frantic effort, and trying with all my might to suppress the urge to laugh, I couldn't help myself. Again and again, I burst out laughing.

I was mortified! As soon the session was over, I went straight to Dr. Van Riper's office.

"I've got to quit the program! I'm a failure! Oh, I'm so ashamed! I couldn't help myself, but I LAUGHED at my patient. I just don't have the discipline to control myself, so I will never be able to help these stutterers. I've got to quit."

"Was it funny?" Dr. Van Riper asked, with a smile.

"It was hilarious!" I replied. "I just burst out laughing–again and again!"

"Then you've got to laugh," my professor said. "Your patient deserves your honest feedback. People are going to laugh at him, He needs to learn not to be intimidated by whatever reaction he gets. He needs to practice pushing ahead and getting his message across, getting the answer he needs, no matter what. He needs to get his need met, whether his attempts are funny to the rest of the world or not."

"Are you sure?"

"Absolutely! Remember, I'm a stutterer myself. I know these things!"

So, I didn't quit my masters program–and apply for welfare–after all. Thank you Dr. Van Riper!

Peter "Smith"

A little three-year-old boy, Peter "Smith", was brought by his mom to Western Michigan for evaluation and treatment. The most obvious thing about Peter was that he was not talking–*at all*!

Most children are saying single words by 12 months and two-word combinations by two years: "More milk!" and "Go bye-bye!" By 36 months, they should be speaking in five- and six-word sentences with 75-100 percent intelligibility–75 to a perfect stranger and 100 percent to the parents. By age four, they should be totally intelligible.

So Peter was brought to the talking experts–the speech pathology department. Dr. Erickson assigned him to me, because "You have three years' experience," he said, and "This will be a very challenging case."

Oh great! Thanks a bunch! I thought.

The information we were given was that Peter was mentally handicapped. When I started working with him, he didn't seem mentally handicapped at all—too much curiosity.

I had gone to school—elementary school—with mentally handicapped kids. Not the kids in *my* class, of course; *we* were not mentally handicapped. Rather, we all had *physical*—muscular and neurological—problems. But, at recess, at lunch, and on the bus we would interact with the kids from the mentally handicapped class. I got to know what mentally handicapped kids were like: they were fun, happy or laughing, but lacking in curiosity.

My Peter Smith, at Western Michigan, was curious about *everything*; he was *into* everything! He was "bright eyed and bushy tailed"—he wanted to *learn*.

There was a psychologist assigned to the Speech Pathology department, a Dr. Sperling. I spoke to Dr. Sperling about my observations. He said, "Well, let's give him an I.Q. test!"

"Who will do that?" I asked.

"You will!"

"What? I'm just a speech pathology student; I don't know anything about giving an I.Q. test!"

"You have a relationship with the child. Rather than have a stranger do it, I will teach you how to do each section, and you will administer the test." So, every week for a while, Dr. Sperling would teach me to administer a couple of sub-tests of the Stanford-Benet IQ test, and I would administer them to Peter.

When it was all over and the scores were in, he tested normal!

I started working with the boy to increase his vocabulary. I learned that his doctor father had a boat and was interested in boats. So I got a plastic sandbox and filled it with water. I bought some toy sailboats, and we played "Boats." We talked about boats this, and boats that. Before long, the mom told me that the father had finally started up a relationship with the boy. She said that I'd utterly saved her son—rescued him. "We thought he was retarded." They had locked him up in his room! And his father was a physician! (Duh.)

In the end, we confirmed in spades that Peter was NOT mentally handicapped at all. He made enormous progress in therapy, and we were all thrilled to watch that progress. After a year of therapy, twice a week, he was doing fine. He left the year of therapy talking in sentences. He was just an adorable child.

I don't know why, but I never saw the father.

The Hines VA Hospital

As the year at Western Michigan neared a close, something life-changing happened for me. Dr. Van Riper said, "We have an internship opportunity for two people, at the Hines Veterans Administration (VA) hospital in Chicago."

There were three of us who were qualified and interested, so Dr. Van Riper had us draw straws. Two of us would get this choice internship, to complete the Master's degree; the remaining one would still have to write a thesis. I hated writing:[22] *What if I have to write a thesis after all?* I thought.

Dr. Van Riper held the straws—and I won one of the two internships!

It was at Hines VA hospital that I learned about *aphasia*, more than anywhere else. I was just bowled

---

[22] My husband and co-author here *loves* to write. Thank goodness. I just tell him my stories, and he does the rest.

over by it. I loved working with the stroke patients and the head injury patients. From then on, I *definitely* wanted to work in a hospital, with the brain-damaged. I filled out a government application form, then known as Form 57–and waited. In late summer, I got notice of some openings for speech and language pathologists at Federal Government hospitals. One was in Philadelphia. Another was in San Antonio. The third was at Walter Reed. *That* was the job I wanted! *(Maybe the President will be treated there again!)* [23]

As I was getting my Master's degree (1965-66), the United States was getting deeper and deeper into the war in Vietnam. More and more soldiers were being badly wounded in that faraway place, and many of the worst cases were being airlifted back to Walter Reed Army Hospital, on their way to other military or Veterans Administration hospitals, or–for the lucky ones–home.

I was thrilled about the possibility of working at Walter Reed, but I was soon also depressed. It had been weeks since I sent in my government application form. Not hearing anything, I had finally signed a year's contract with the Rochester public schools, and the school year was about to begin.

I thought that, if I went back on my word, no one would ever hire me again. I really wanted that Walter Reed job, but I was under contract to Rochester. I wrote and asked my mentor, Dr. Van Riper, head of Speech-Language Pathology at Western Michigan, what I should do. He said, "If this is really what you want to do, break your contract. Quit Rochester and take the job at Walter Reed."

[23] See chapter: "**Walter Reed**."

I couldn't. I had given my word. I couldn't just throw it away like an empty candy wrapper. With tears in my heart, I moved on and focused my mind on my job in Rochester.

Months later, as I was finishing up the school year in Rochester, I got a letter. The Walter Reed position was still open; was I interested? *Was I interested?!* My mother and I flew to Washington the following week, for my interview!

At Walter Reed, my mother stayed in our rental car,[24] while I entered the main hospital building for my interview. I reported to the Human Resources office, and the woman I spoke to there drove me to the Forest Glen Annex a few miles away, to interview with the Supervisor of the Speech-Language Section, Mr. Bill Simpkins.

During the interview, a woman named Blanche Schnapper happened into the room, and Mr. Simpkins introduced me. Miss Schnapper asked if I liked working with stutterers, and I said, "Oh, yes!" Simpkins said, "She studied with Professor Van Riper," to which Blanche said, firmly and loudly—"Hire her!"

As the interview was winding down, I passed on a message: "Miss Smyth in Personnel said she wants you to call her when the interview is done, because she needs to know your decision." I learned later that Mr. Simpkins was a notorious procrastinator. I suppose Miss Smyth knew it, and that may have been the reason for her message. Who knows, it may also have been the reason why the position was still open!

---

[24] What a Mom! As always, she was *there*, discreetly out of sight, as I sought this very important *professional* position!

65

Anyway, to my complete surprise, as I sat there, Mr. Simpkins picked up the phone, called Miss Smyth,[25] and in my presence said, "I've decided to hire Miss Silverwood."

"You did?!!" my mother screamed–back at our parked car–when I told her, "I got the job!"

The next few days were a whirlwind. We rented an apartment on Connecticut Avenue, on my cousin Sara's advice that the area was a safe place for me to live. Then we flew back to Chicago so I could move to Washington D.C.!

Soon enough, I had my clothes packed and loaded into my little Chevy Corvair, along with a folding cot, a card table and a lawn chair. Those would be my furniture while I was getting settled in Washington. Then I drove to Washington alone and reported to work–July 5, 1967–at my DREAM JOB!

[25] This name has been changed.

A GIRL'S LIFE AT WALTER REED

"Ask not what your country can do for you;
ask what you can do for your country."
−President John F. Kennedy; 1961 inaugural address.

The Patients Of Walter Reed

When I had been at the V.A. hospital, for my internship near the end of my Masters degree program, we had seen every sort of patient, both ambulatory and non-ambulatory. But at Walter Reed we were just seeing the ambulatory patients−those who could ride a military bus to the Speech and Audiology office at the Forest Glen Annex, about four miles from the main hospital campus. After a few months of that, I said to my boss, Bill Simpkins, "What do you think about my working at the main hospital, to see the patients who cannot get here to the ambulatory center?" He said, "But, we don't have an office for you there."

I said, "I don't care. I will just go from bed to bed and ward to ward, carrying my equipment with me. Those patients need our services."

Bill said, "Fine, go ahead."

So for many months, I "plied my trade" at the main hospital building, going from bed to bed and ward to ward carrying my heavy old (1960s) audio tape-recorder and my equally heavy *Language Master* with me. Finally, after about six months of this, I said to the head of neurology, "I cannot do this any more; I need an office." Within 24 hours he got me one.

So, after that, I was in the office that I was given by the head of neurology. It was huge; it was bigger than a master bedroom.

Vietnam Memories

My new office was very close to the unlocked psychiatric ward. One day, two soldiers walked into my office and introduced themselves.

"We just got here," they said. They had just arrived by airplane from Vietnam, probably by way of Frankfort, Germany.

"I'm glad you're here," I said.

We chatted amiably for a while, and then they left.

A little while after they had gone, one of them returned. At first I thought he was going to flirt with me, or ask me out. Instead, he said to me, "Could I talk with you some more? Do you have the time?"

"Sure," I replied.

"I just need to talk to someone about what happened—what I did—in 'Nam."

I guess the earlier talking helped him somehow; maybe I just seemed a good listener. Of course, I was a young woman, and all of the psychologists were men.

I didn't know why he was at Walter Reed; we would never have asked any patient about that if we didn't have an official reason to inquire; they might have been in for some highly personal reason that was none of our business.

Well, he told me that, back in Vietnam, he had pushed a prisoner out of a helicopter, to his death. I don't know whether he was ordered to do that, but he was psychologically destroyed by having done it. I was the first person other than military people that he had seen since the incident, so maybe he felt he could talk to me without fear of discipline. Just before he left, he said that I was the first person with whom he had been able to talk about his haunting experience.

So, there were times when I was not just a speech pathologist, but I was like an ad hoc psychologist−or at least a sympathetic ear. This happened more than once. I think there was something about my being a woman−a young civilian woman.... The guys seemed to feel that talking to me, perhaps the first civilian woman they had encountered since returning from the war, was like talking to a trusted family member more than to someone militarily official.

After the first time, I would leave my door open, if I could−so that, for patients who needed to talk, I could be available. These two I've just discussed may have been the first. I probably started leaving my door open after that.

I don't remember doing any flirting at Walter Reed. Well... there was one guy I liked a lot. He worked there. I didn't flirt with the patients at all; I joked with them and had fun. (They may have *thought* I was flirting.) I tried to make them feel at home. I realized that they needed to know that a woman could still talk and relate to them, even if they'd lost both legs, for instance. That kind of thing. I was really invested in my job at that time there.

I don't think I ever dated a patient. Walter Reed is an acute hospital, so as soon as possible, the patients are sent to another Army (or Veterans Administration) hospital. I didn't meet the ambulatory speech patients very much, they went out to the outpatient clinic at the Forest Glen Annex.

I did a lot of work on the neuro-surgery ward. Most of the patients on that ward, with paralysis, had beds with a hole in the mattress, where their pillow would have been, so they could lie on their stomach and breathe through the hole. The nurses would flip them over every so often, to prevent bedsores. Sometimes I would get down and sit on the floor, so I could converse with them. I was sitting—not lying!—on the floor. (I always tried to be very professional!) But I kept up a lot of conversation with the guys. Here you are, at Walter Reed hospital. Alone. Disabled. Suddenly separated from your unit in the field—not to mention your family and friends. It's a situation made for depression.

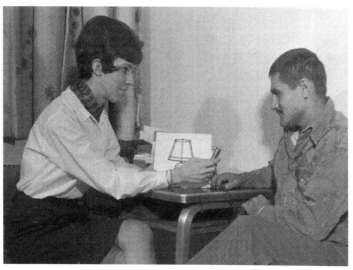

With a patient, in my office.

I think that when the guys met me–perhaps the first young American civilian woman they had encountered since leaving the war zone–it was beneficial to them to discover that a young woman would still at least just talk to them, however broken in body they were, whatever body part might now be missing, compared to the condition of robust health and vigor in which they had deployed from their American homeland so recently.

Moving around the hospital, I constantly said to myself–*Don't look shocked! Stay calm!* I would never know what grotesque horror might be coming around the corner. At times it was really hard. Some had part of their head shot off–gone. Some had no eye; some were terribly scarred–deformed even. We saw just about everything, except for severe burns. Burn patients went to the Burn Center at the U.S Army Institute of Surgical Research, Brooke Army Hospital, Fort Sam Houston, Texas.

Some Unwanted Attention

Coming back from lunch one day, I stepped into the elevator from the 1st floor to return to my office on the 3rd floor. When the elevator stopped at the second floor, three young soldiers entered, none of whom I had ever seen. I guessed that they were just back from Vietnam. Their appearance was normal, fairly nice looking; and they were ambulatory, with no obvious physical wounds.

As they entered the elevator, one of them–sort of flirtatiously–said, "Well! *Hello there!*" Then, the one who was nearest the controls stopped the elevator between the floors and–more threateningly–said, "Now we gotcha where we want you!" and laughed, leeringly!

I thought, *My life is over.* The other two were grinning and laughing and digging it. I thought, *I can't wrestle them for the controls, I just need to talk my way out of this.*

I didn't smile or laugh, and I became very serious. "This isn't funny, guys." I said. Thank goodness I was wearing my white lab coat, looking a little like a doctor (I hoped).

It must have been only about a minute or two, but it seemed like a year and a half. Finally I said, in the most confident tone I could muster, "O.K. guys, enough is enough—I've got a meeting to go to. You're holding me up. Let's go!"

They probably were pretty normal guys, just over the line a little in the teasing mode. They probably hadn't seen many women for a long time, and they were certainly enjoying their little game. At least I *hoped* it was a little game.

Finally, seeing I was neither showing fear nor appearing at all entertained, they gave up, re-started the elevator, and let me go. I had been outwardly calm and professional throughout, but when I got back to my desk, my heart was pounding! I was a wreck!

I had not seen any of the three guys before, and I never saw them afterward. I don't know what their reasons were to be at Walter Reed. They were probably assigned to my building for either neurology or psychology concerns. They may have been among those psych patients who were not confined to a locked ward.

A Close Call

Another time, I had a patient who had just come back from Vietnam with probable PTSD,[26] who seemed to have a lot of anger. He was not especially angry at me, but angry at everything and everyone. After my first session with him, I went to see one of the psychologists—whose office was nearby in the neuro-psych building where my office was also located. I said, "I have a concern about the level of anger this man is exhibiting. He needs some support that I don't feel qualified to give." I asked the psychologist, "Would you be willing to just come and sit in on my next session with him?"

Next day the psychologist came and joined the session. He sat between me and the patient. The patient was as angry as ever. The psychologist began to talk with him, and the patient responded by drawing a knife!

I had never seen anyone pull a knife before. I was thinking—*We are going to die!*

The psychologist kept his cool and continued to engage the patient in conversation,. At some point the psychologist casually reached over to a box of tissue and took about half of the box as padding—in case he had to lunge for the knife! With a pad of tissue as armor! I was torn between going for help and staying in the scene. I didn't want to leave the psychologist alone. The patient *knew* me, at least a little. He didn't know the psychologist at all. *Maybe if I am here, it will be calmer* I thought.

[26] Post-traumatic stress disorder

73

The psychologist was masterful at talking him down and getting him to relax. Finally—after a seeming eternity—the patient put the knife down.

The next thing that happened was that the patient was admitted to a locked ward. I never saw him again. Clearly, he had problems that went way beyond any speech problem he may have had!

Public Speaking

Early in my career at Walter Reed, I was asked to give a talk to a group of young doctors about Speech Pathology. Most of them, I knew, would have little interest in my subject, but they were required to attend a particular lecture series as part of their training. Well, any form of public speaking had always held pure terror for me. But I swallowed hard and agreed to do it.

Came the morning of my lecture, and I was terrified. When I was introduced, I stepped, trembling, upon the podium, a sheaf of notes in my hand. I started speaking.

After a few seconds, I sensed something was wrong. The lectern seemed to be growing, moving before my eyes. *Isn't that funny* I thought. *I am so nervous that I am experiencing an hallucination. My anxiety has caused an alteration of my visual field. I feel as if I am shrinking in stature before these august young doctors. I have never felt so small (or so nervous).*

Not wanting to miss a beat, I kept talking, but the effect continued. Bigger and bigger seemed the lectern. Smaller and smaller I felt in my body. *This cannot possibly be happening. I am so nervous that it seems as if this lectern is actually in motion.*

Finally, I could stand it no longer. I had now shrunk to the point where I could no longer see over the lectern, and my audience was now hidden from me.

"HELLO?" I said aloud–for the first time acknowledging to my audience what was happening to me. A roar of laughter!

I was so nervous that I was leaning hard on the lectern and, unbeknownst to me, I was bearing down on a button that activated a motor in the lectern that was meant to raise or lower the lectern for speakers of varying stature. There I was, Pam Silverwood, now speaking from a lectern meant for Michael Jordan or Manute Bol![27]

A Night Out With "A Patient"

The Welfare and Recreation Office was located right around the corner from my office. In my free moments, I would be there talking to Connie Laws. She frequently arranged for me to accompany groups of patients to recreational events: concerts, such as Frank Sinatra or recreational activities such as ocean fishing or skiing. One day, two tickets to a concert at the Kennedy Center came in, late. Connie said to me, "These tickets just came in today, for tonight. I can't find any patients who can go. Do you know someone who can use these tickets with you?" I was sure my friend, Mary Modderman, would be up for it. "Just one thing," Connie said. "These tickets are donated by a concert patron, who may be sitting next to you, so be

[27] Manute Bol was a Sudanese-born American basketball player and political activist. Listed at 7 ft. 7 in tall, he was the tallest player in the history of the National Basketball Association, along with Gheorghe Mureşan. Bol was active in the NBA from 1985 to 1995.

sure your friend can act like a patient." Well, Mary is an occupational therapist who works with patients all the time—she's lots of fun and she's game for anything—so I knew that Mary could pull it off.

So we went to the Kennedy Center Concert Hall, and I guided Mary into the Concert Hall and to our seats. As luck would have it, the ticket donors were sitting right behind us. So I whispered that information to Mary and she did a super job pretending to be a patient.

Connie Laws did a lot of things to make Walter Reed a fun place to be. Celebrity performers who visited the hospital from time to time included Bob Hope, Rod McEwen and Ed Sullivan. Connie would be in charge of hosting the performers.

"Would you be Bob Hope's assistant, Pam." Would I ?! So I sat in Bob Hope's dressing room one night, as his gofer. He never asked me to do anything, except maybe to get him a drink of water. I made bold to ask him "What is Bing Crosby really like?
Mr. Hope made a really funny crack, something like, "Well, he's a lousy golfer." Hope had a golf club with him, and he would swing it just to relax. (I wonder if that's where Johnny Carson got his famous pantomimed golf swing, with which he usually terminated his opening monologue on NBC's *The Tonight Show*.) He was not overly impressed with himself; a super nice person. When he was not on stage, he was not "on." Usually he was with other guests.

As Bob Hope's gofer for a day, I made myself as useful as I could, but mostly stayed in the background.

A Ski Trip

One time, Connie asked me to accompany a group of patients on a ski trip. I hadn't learned to walk until I was two, so I certainly had never been skiing. I thought, "If I'm ever going to go skiing, this is the time to go. If these patients can ski on one leg, I should be able to ski with two!" Famous last words!

Poised for the slalom race.

I took a skiing lesson, and then started out on the beginners' slope. Later, we had a slalom race. I managed that without mishap, so someone suggested I move on to the intermediate run. Bad choice. Almost 3/4 of the way to the bottom of the intermediate run, where the slope was leveling out, I just fell over and heard a muffled cracking sound.

I had previously met some of the ski patrol, and, as it happened, one came up right behind me and said, "Fancy meeting you here. How are you doing?"

"I just broke my leg," I said.

"How do you know."

"I heard it CRACK!"

Some of my group drove me to the hospital; I was in the back, Bill Demby was in the front, with another guy driving. Believe it or not, the driver stopped to feed some birds along the way. I couldn't believe it!

"Now let me get this straight," I said. "I've just broken my leg. We're on our way to the hospital, to set my leg—and you're feeding the birds?"

"Well," he said, "the birds have to eat."

I was in a hurry, not only because my leg was broken, but also—I was having a call of nature! When we finally got to the hospital, I had to go to the bathroom, broken leg and all, before I could get any treatment. That was awkward.

My leg hurt like heck. "Will I ever walk again?" I asked the doctor. Since I didn't learn to walk until I was two, and I still walked with a limp, I was very concerned.

"I can't guarantee that," the doctor said.

Oh, great; just the assurance I need!

Back home from the ski trip, with a leg cast and crutches, I couldn't live in my walk-up apartment, alone. So I stayed for a while with my friend Mary. Then I moved in with my brother Jim and his wife, for a time. They had just recently been married, and I didn't like imposing on them. Finally I was able to go back to my apartment. Once I could get up the stairs and into my apartment, I was fine.

Next, I went back to work at Walter Reed. After they gave me a cast that let me bend my knee, I could drive myself to the hospital–using my left leg only, if you can picture that! Once there, I could get into a wheelchair. If I couldn't get to some of the wards–the stairs again–someone would bring the patients to me.

But, while wheeling myself from ward to ward, wearing my white lab coat–with a briefcase on my lap and an enormous cast sticking out in front like a battering ram–the Commanding General, General Bernstein, saw me the first day back and said "Now that is dedication. Here   you are in a leg cast and a wheelchair, and you've come to work regardless! I am impressed!"

Sometimes, an ambulatory patient would offer to push my wheelchair. Picture that! They were thrilled to do it! It gave them a purpose and sort of restored a piece of their identity to be useful by helping me, the helper, to get around to see my other patients!

Well, that is the story of my first ski trip; I went skiing, as the only one in the party with two flesh-and-blood legs, and I was the only one to be driven to the hospital with an injury. I was the only one who broke a leg! I don't know how or why it happened, so I'd never know how to avoid it in the future.

I never went skiing again.

Ocean Fishing

In the Spring or summer of '82, the year I was married, Connie asked me to go ocean fishing with a group. When I got my first fish on the line, I said "I can't get it in!" But the captain was right behind me, and he said "Oh, yes you can!" I realized then, how tough it was, what a challenge it was to get those big fish into the boat. I caught about eight fish myself, but the patients I was with, having no way to keep or cook the fish, gave me theirs. So I came home to David—with 18 or so BIG bluefish to clean.

As we worked, David said, "I'm not doing a very professional job of this; I'm wasting a lot of the flesh."

"It's not like we have a shortage," I said, "Just get it done." From those big fish, out on our porch in the dark, we cut six or more big filets per fish, 121 servings in all. We saved a lot of money (and we didn't lose very many friends)! Two years later, I was still inviting my friends over for bluefish dinners. My friend, Ed Yoe, once said, "I'll come, but only if you're not serving Bluefish!"

"We'd Like You To See Another Patient!"

It was an ordinary day, early morning, I was going up the stairs to see a patient on the ward. I opened one of the two big frosted glass doors to the ward, and there were two young doctors—one on each side of the door—waiting, as if they'd known I was coming. In a flash, they had me off the ground, carrying me by the shoulders and elbows, one on each side, my feet flailing in the air—they, talking, all the way down the hall!

"We know you're the best speech pathologist on the planet," one said. "If anyone can get this patient talking, it's you! He's had some problems: kidney failure, heart not doing real well."

I always wanted to greet each patient by name, so as we rounded the corner, I looked to read the name plaque beside the door—but there was no name there! *OmiGod,* I realized—*he's dead!* They put me down inside the door—and they *ran*—leaving me with a corpse!!

Many years later, one of those young doctors became the Commanding General of Walter Reed.[28] More on that in the chapter, "A New Beginning."

---

[28]Lieutenant General Ronald R. Blanck, D.O., (U.S. Army, retired). Dr. Blanck began his military career in 1968 as a medical officer and battalion surgeon in Vietnam. He retired 32 years later as the Surgeon General of the U.S. Army and commander of the U.S. Army Medical Command, with more than 46,000 military personnel and 26,000 civilian employees throughout the world.

During his distinguished military career, Dr. Blanck also served as commander of the Walter Reed Army Medical Center; the North Atlantic Region Medical Command; and as the Director of Professional Services and Chief of Medical Corps Affairs for the U.S. Army Surgeon General. Other assignments included Assistant Dean of Student Affairs at the Uniformed Services University School of Medicine; Chief of the Department of Medicine at Brooke Army Medical Center; Commander of the Berlin Army Hospital; and Commander, Frankfurt Regional Army Medical Center.

Dr. Blanck's military honors include Distinguished Service Medals, the Defense Superior Service Medal, the Legion of Merit,

Mamie Eisenhower

Former First Lady Mamie Eisenhower–retired with President "Ike," at their Gettysburg farm–had a severe stroke. She was admitted for treatment at Walter Reed. Soon after, I happened to encounter the Chief of Neurology in the elevator. (More about him, in a minute.) "How is Mrs. Eisenhower doing," I asked. "Well, she's had a pretty severe stroke. Do you want to see her?"

"Certainly–if she has a speech-language problem."

"I'll send you a consult." In other words, a written request to consult, to see a particular patient and perhaps to treat, but in any case to report back one's findings.

Next morning, I got the consult from Dr. Huott.

Dr. Huott was then the Chief of Neurology, but years before, I'd had a run-in with him. I had just been assigned an office, right in the midst of all the neurologists in the psycho-neurology section. Dr. Huott–then merely the *Assistant* Chief of Neurology–told me, "If I were head of this department, you wouldn't have that office."

"Maybe that's why you're not the head of the department," I quipped. Dr. Huott smiled slightly, as if to say, "You got me."

Thanks, Tom, I thought. Years of growing up with my "big" brother, Tom, had tempered and toughened me, so when it came to withstanding and

the Bronze Star, the Meritorious Service Medal, and the Army Commendation Medal. –*Wikipedia, retrieved May 21, 2014*

reacting quickly to barbs and challenges from older males, I was ready!

Now, years later, Dr. Huott was the Chief of Neurology, and he had become accustomed enough to my presence that he was going to send me to evaluate and treat the former First Lady of the United States. Not that he *initiated* the thought to have me consult on the case, of course. Except for a chance meeting in the elevator, who knows when or whether Mrs. Eisenhower would have received speech therapy services, though she proved to have severe speech deficits resulting from her recent stroke. Perhaps, as some doctors do, and although he was the attending physician in her case, Dr. Huott was going about his business treating her from the perspective of his specialty alone, without imagining that a non-medical professional might be essential to the fullest treatment of a medical case!

So, next morning, I went to see Mrs. Eisenhower, way up on the seventh floor in ward 72, the V.I.P. ward. This was a highly secured area, with a locked door. I pushed the button, and someone came to the door to let me in. I went to the head nurse, at her desk, and I said, "I'm Pam Silverwood from Speech Pathology; I'm here to see Mrs. Eisenhower." She took me to the door and asked me to wait while she checked to ensure that the patient was "decent" and ready to see me.

While waiting, I noticed some kind of tall, wooden sculpture, just outside the door. This I later learned had been donated to the V.I.P. ward by some high official of Thailand, perhaps even the head of Thailand—President, Prime Minister, whatever. As I bent down to read the inscription on the plaque, I crashed my forehead on some sharp protrusion of this totemic object, and immediately I began to see stars.

"Come in, Miss Silverwood," said the head nurse. "Mrs. Eisenhower will see you now."

Awed as I was at the prospect of seeing a First Lady, I didn't have the sense to say, "One moment, please. I've just bumped my head, and I need to gather my senses a bit." No, I practically bolted through the door, certainly not wanting to keep my V.I.P. patient waiting. The head nurse introduced me and my purpose, then gracefully excused herself.

"Good morning, Mrs. Eisenhower," I said. "How are you feeling this morning?" There she was, sitting up in bed, neatly attired in a pink dressing gown, with her famous bangs well coiffed.

Her response was reserved; a bit cool, I thought. Also, she was clearly seriously impaired—a little "out of it," it seemed—with very little ability to verbalize. Clearly, she liked the color pink. There was pink this and pink that, all around the room, including two vases of pink flowers. There was even a pink tray-table, provenance unknown. Perhaps that had been brought in for her from her home, I didn't know. Maybe someone had quickly arranged for the paint shop to customize it for her within the 24-48 hours since she had arrived. She was certainly being treated like the V.I.P. she was—the wife of a *Five*-Star, *General of the Army,* and former President. No comfort was to be spared.

During our first conversation, she seemed to warm up to me, and we began to develop a comfortable and cordial relationship. After I got to know her a little better, after a couple of visits, we would play cards—part of her therapy, of course.

Now, at this point, you may want to know: was it Poker or Gin Rummy? Bridge or Hearts? After all these years, I confess, I cannot remember. I was, of course, thinking about her condition and progress. Through all my visits with her, I was subtly—in my oblique way—"testing" the daylights out of her, looking for signs of progress and not seeing much. Maybe I was also, still, a little in awe of being at cards with the Secret Service and a First Lady of The United States. (If my mother could see me now.) Of course, it wasn't the card game itself that was meant to be the most therapeutic. I enlisted the Secret Service Agents at the table to help encourage her speech, by asking her leading questions, for the purpose of motivating her efforts to speak.

She made very little progress. She had suffered a massive stroke. I had seen her for about a month when, one morning, she seemed to be declining. Nevertheless, as I was leaving, she pressed a small wine glass into my hand, indicating that she wanted me to have it. Outside her room, I offered it to her Secret Service Agent: "She gave this to me," I said. "You'd better take it." I was mindful that, somewhere, there were regulations about government employees taking gifts, in the performance of their duties. I didn't know if they applied to me; but I wasn't taking any chances.

"Did she give it to you?"

I nodded.

"If Mamie Eisenhower gives you something, she wants you to have it."

I'm sure that some of those Secret Service Agents had been assigned to Mrs. Eisenhower for years. They must have known her well.

At the nurses' station, I wrote into the chart that her condition was worsening, that I was concerned for her well being; then I asked a nurse if they had seen as much. They had not. *Well, it's subtle*, I thought.

Next day, before I saw her again, she died. I still have that little wine glass. It is one of my prized possessions. Later, I sent a sympathy card to Mrs. Eisenhower's son, John Eisenhower, who graciously replied to me.

John S D Eisenhower
Valley Forge, Pennsylvania 19481

December 15, 1979

Ms. Pamela Silverwood
9284 Adelphi Road
Adelphi, MD 20783

Dear Pam:

Many thanks for your card and your nice note. Although you did know Mother only a short time, as you say, I was quite impressed by your understanding and your zeal to restore her speech despite the fact that it looked to be an impossible task.

I am unable to express my appreciation of everything done for Mother at Walter Reed. Although the death of a loved one is difficult, it is certainly mixed with a warm feeling of gratitude.

I hope that our paths cross again.

Sincerely,

John Eisenhower

JSDEisenhower/jah

U.S. Senator Karl E. Mundt

My treatment of Senator Mundt is detailed in the Prologue. The Senator had suffered a severe stroke in November 1969, for which he was treated at Walter Reed. I treated him for speech, for about six months–during which time he made no progress at all. I discharged him from speech therapy sometime in 1970. He also received extensive physical therapy. His wife, Mary, led his staff in Mundt's place and refused calls for the crippled Senator to resign. Mundt was stripped of his committee assignments by the Senate Republican Conference in 1972. He did not seek reelection in 1972, but he remained in office through the end of his term on January 3, 1973. He died in Washington, D.C., August 16, 1974, of a heart ailment.[29]

Bill Demby

I met a lot of patients who were not speech patients, through Connie Laws, who was the head of patient Welfare and Recreation. She frequently asked me to join patient groups, on all kinds of trips and excursions arranged by her office. My office was close to hers, and I would often stop in and say hello. One such time, there was a patient sitting there in her office, socializing, gadding about the hospital while trying out his brand new prosthetic legs. And thus I met Bill Demby.

Somehow, in the midst of all the hilarity of meeting Bill for the first time, he bragged that, now that he had legs, he also−for the first time in a long time−had a lap. Wanting to try out also his new lap, he wondered whether I might like to sit for awhile on his lap.

Taken aback only for a moment, I replied, "Well, I would, but I'm afraid I might get splinters!"

Well, that pretty well broke everyone up, and my friendship with Mr. Bill Demby was off to a rollicking start. I was super impressed with Bill's ability to manage his handicap, and we seemed to share a sense of humor that just clicked.

[29] https://en.wikipedia.org/wiki/Karl_E._Mundt Retrieved February 5, 2017.

Bill was a real gadabout. He had a reputation, even before he got his legs, for running about the hospital in a wheelchair—socializing. You could never find him; he was never on his ward. One time, he found a letter left on his pillow that said, "Dear Bill, If you could find some time in your social calendar, I would love to meet up with you sometime. —Your Physician."

Bill sometimes invited me into the group he gathered around himself—for instance, on the infamous ski trip, when I broke my leg in the company of a group of amputees, each of whom retained only one natural leg (or perhaps none) to break.

Another time, Bill and some fellow amputees were horsing around in the snow, in Rock Creek Park. At someone's instigation (probably Bill's) the group arranged some of their prosthetic legs and arms in the snow—sticking out of a snow bank—and then hid in a car and watched with amusement the passing motorists' panicked reactions to the contrived scene of horror.

Bill later did a lot of public service work, and he was eventually seen in a certain public service TV commercial, playing basketball on his twin prosthetic legs—putting an effective move on a very surprised opposing player, who was wearing only the legs he was born with. I well remember Bill's self-satisfied grin at the end of that commercial—having put one over on the unsuspecting other guy.

"Mother-In-Law"

One soldier had had part of his head chopped off by a helicopter blade. He had no speech at all, beyond saying "Uh-huh and Uh-Uh." I would get him singing, "Twinkle-Twinkle Little Star, Row Row your boat and such. He would almost immediately get the tune and hum or sing the tune. He was surprised, with a happy face, when finally the words started coming out. I took him to the ward, where the nurse said, "I wish you could get him to say his wife's and mother-in-law's names. They're coming to see him next weekend."

There was a pop song then, called *Mother-In-Law*, which I undertook to learn and teach him. When his wife and mother-in-law came to visit, I was not on the ward; it was over a weekend. So, I had wondered, how did he do? The head nurse said that, when he saw them, he broke into the song immediately—and there wasn't a dry eye on the ward!

General Lewis B. Hershey

General Lewis B. Hershey may be best known, to generations of draft-eligible males, as the director of the Selective Service Administration; he was also very active in the Boy Scouts of America. General Hershey's wife died while the general was in the hospital following a stroke. I asked of him, "What can I do for you?"

"I want you to come to the funeral with me."

"I will be happy to do that, if that will be helpful to you."

At the funeral, I said, "Where do you want me to be."

"Right here next to me."

General Hershey had made pretty good progress in therapy, up to that point. But he was insecure. That is why he wanted me to sit next to him, in case he got into any kind of communicative trouble. But he did just fine.

He greeted people, and they talked, and he responded appropriately. I didn't have to say much. As to whether anyone may have wondered who his twenty-something companion was, he simply introduced me as his speech therapist, and that was that.

My "Miracle Cure"

I once had a patient, a drill sergeant, who could not speak. I don't know what sort of trauma may have caused his loss of voice, but it was not physiological—it was definitely *psycho*logical.[30] How do I know? Because I was able to "talk him out of it."

He came to my office, and after a few introductory formalities, I said,

"I understand that you've lost the ability to speak."

He nodded.

I said, "OK, before we get started, I want you to just clear your throat—just get anything out of there that may be in the way."

"Hhh-r-r-r-a-a-a-a-a-a-k-k-k."

Once he did that, I said, "Now that is voice."

"OK, so we know you can make sound!"

I had essentially *tricked* him into demonstrating that his vocal cords were in working order. With that established, I very gently, carefully and slowly assured him that, "You don't have to use your voice anyplace but here, until you are ready."

"Are you ready to do it again, just right here?

---

[30] The condition is called *hysterical aphonia*.

He nodded.

"OK, now I want you to just close your mouth and clear you throat again, but then go right into a Hummm."

"Hrrak-mmmmmmm."

"Now just do the 'Hmmmm' part again."

"Hum-m-m."

"OK, do it again, and make it last a little longer. "

"Hm-m-m-m-m-m-m-m-m-m-m-m-m-m."

"OK, do it again, and this time, open your mouth towards the end of the sound, but keep it going."

"Hm-m-m-m-m-m-m-m-m-m-m-m-a-a-a-a."

"OK, you just said, Ma." Can you do it again, but this time, at the very end just open your mouth up again."

"Hm-m-m-m-m-m-m-m-m-m-mm-a-a-a-a-m-m.

Well, you just said "Mom." What do you think of that? Now, you don't ever have to use that anywhere outside this room, until you're ready. Are you comfortable with that?

He nodded again.

We worked liked that for several minutes, gradually expanding the range of words that he could say. When he was talking almost normally, I asked him whether he was ready to try out his restored voice on someone other than myself.

He nodded once more.

"OK, lets go out and find someone to talk to." Is there someone on your ward with whom you'd feel comfortable talking?"

(A shrug.)

"Would you be comfortable just saying hello to one of he nurses?"

"Mmm-hmmm."

So I walked him back to his ward, and the head nurse was astounded, when he just said "Hello."

That was our first (and our last) therapy session. *My miracle cure!* I just said to him, "I'm here. You can come back and talk to me any time you want, if you have any trouble again, or if you just want to let me know how you're doing." OK?

"Mmmmm-hmmmm."

I also let him know that I was going to refer him to talk to psychology about his situation. I knew from my graduate courses that—as Dr. Freud had taught the world—if his loss of voice had a psychological origin, once that adaptation was no longer available to him, whatever problem underlay his going mute would be likely to crop up in the form of some other "adaptation," perhaps one even less appropriate for his future success in life than going mute.

He did come back to see me once or twice, and evidently he was getting along just fine the last time I saw him. He was very happy with his progress.

Justice William O. Douglas

.   One day, as I was visiting the physical therapy department, on business, I encountered U.S. Supreme

Court Justice William O. Douglas, sitting alone in his wheelchair. He was in the hospital following a stroke, which had left him impaired as to both speech and walking.[31] As it happened, my next appointment was with the Justice himself, so I said

"Good morning, Justice Douglas. Are you ready for your speech appointment?"   "Yes," he nodded, with a smile. So I seized the handles of his wheelchair and whisked him away to my office.

Later, as I was about to wrap up my session with the Justice, my telephone rang.

"I'm sorry, Miss Silverwood! I know that Justice Douglas was due for his appointment almost an hour ago, but *we can't find him!* When we went to get him from his appointment at Physical Therapy, he had simply disappeared! Physical Therapy didn't know where he had gone! We're still searching all over the hospital for him, but he's just gone! Hospital Security is on the phone with the FBI, right now, to report him as missing! We don't know what to do!" We're frantic here!

I leave my embarrassment, in the rest of the conversation, to your imagination.

---

[31] Justice Douglas, though of advanced years, was a frequent hiker. So, the loss of his ability to walk, an effect of his stroke, was a significant tragedy for him. He was well-known for hiking the Chesapeake and Ohio (C&O) Canal trail. He once took a group of reporters along with him as part of his (ultimately successful) campaign to persuade the U.S. Government to restore the Canal and its towpath–a mule trail parallel to the Canal–as a national park.

"Gladys"

One day, between cases, I turned in for a pit stop at the Ladies Room. I was startled to encounter there a lady of middle age, standing at the wash counter, dabbing her eyes, trying to collect herself. She was clearly disturbed about something very serious.

"Is there something I can do to help," I offered.

"Oh, thank you. I don't want to bother you. I just got some bad news from my doctor."

"Please let me help—if I can."

"I just learned that I have a terminal disease," she said with tears in her eyes, "and I'm afraid to die!"

"What are you most afraid of? Leaving others behind?

"No, not really; I - I just don't know what comes next. What will happen to me in the next life. If there is one."

"I understand completely. People have told me a lot of things, since I was a little girl, about what happens to one after one dies. Sometimes, I'm not sure what to believe either."

"It's just such a big unknown. Going into the unknown is really scary. I feel so out of control. I've always been able to control things in my life. But, thinking about dying, it's like stumbling into a big haunted house. What's around the corner. I'm just so afraid."

"Well, I've thought about that some too. Let me ask you a question. What was it like before you were born? Was it scary then?"

"No, there was nothing at all then. It wasn't even a big blank. There was nothing at all; maybe not even a me."

"Did you–do you–have any problem with the way things were then?"

"Well, no; not at all. There weren't any things to afraid of. It was nothing."

"Well, just think about this, then, as a possibility. Could it be that what it is like after life is the same as it was like before life? Maybe life is all there is; maybe there isn't anything either before or after it. I'm not saying that's so; I'm just saying that it *may* be so. There may be nothing to worry about after life, because there may be nothing at all after life... good, bad, or anything."

"Oh my gosh! That is so comforting! I never thought about it that way. Everybody says there's something after life, something to hope for–or to fear. If there is nothing at all–if it's just the way it was before I was born–well that's nothing to worry about. I never regretted anything, all my life, about what came before my life. Maybe there's nothing to regret or worry about after life either."

"Well, just turn that thought over a bit; that's what I do. That's a possibility, it seems, and as long as it's a possibility, that's what I'd like to think about. Excuse me now; I came in here on some business, and I think I'd better take care of it now, before I *do* have something to worry about. Then I have to see a patient in about ten minutes. Will you be OK?

"Thank you so much! You've given me a whole new way to look at it. I'm going to think about what you

97

said. I hope my friends will be as understanding as you have been. What is your name, anyway?"

"My name is Pam. If you see me again around the hospital, please stop me and say hello. My office is just around the corner from here. As long as I'm not with a patient, come in and visit with me, any time."

"Oh, thank you, Pam. My name is Gladys. I'll look for you the next time I'm in the hospital. I never thought I'd find such interesting conversation, *in the ladies room*!" I was feeling so alone, but I think I can drive myself home now. I'll see you again."

I never did see her again, but I hope she found some peace.

Cleft Palate Clinic

Early in my tenure at Walter Reed, I was invited by the head of plastic surgery to attend and contribute to an activity known as Cleft Palate Clinic. You may never have seen a child—certainly not an adult—with an unrepaired cleft palate. In the United States, babies born with cleft palates and/or cleft lips typically undergo reparative surgery within days, to alter what is often an extremely disfigured appearance. In some other countries, many cases go unrepaired, and such children are often hidden by their families from the public. When seen in public, they are often targets of derision and overwhelming discrimination. It's a shame that people can be so cruel to others.

Once or twice a month at Walter Reed, the various medical specialties—those that would be involved in secondary treatment of children born with the cleft palate syndrome—held a clinic to consider what further treatment, if any, should be undertaken. In the morning, having been referred by at least one of the specialties, each parent would bring their child in to a series of appointments, one with each specialty: dentistry, plastic surgery, oral surgery, otolaryngology, social work, speech pathology, audiology, prosthodontics, etc.

In the afternoon, the group of medical and rehabilitative specialists would come together to discuss and reach a consensus recommendation pertaining to each individual child. Once each consensus had been reached, the child's parents would be invited into the room to hear the Clinic's recommendation for a course of action and treatment.

The age range of the patients was from a few months to adult. The range of conditions was from a minimal cleft lip to a highly involved, bi-lateral combination cleft-lip and cleft-palate, with major implications for speech and vocal resonance and hearing, and possible further cosmetic considerations.

When I became Supervisor of the Speech Pathology section, I made sure that I continued participating in the Cleft Palate Clinic, because I *loved* doing it, and I could spare the time, because it was very scheduled and limited; it did not interfere with my management duties, so I assigned it to myself. It gave me an opportunity for a break from management duties and to do something different, that I really enjoyed. I also felt that I was making an important difference, because I finally realized that the vast majority of times that the doctors did surgery on a kid was because of a speech problem, and as a result of my analysis and recommendation. That was very significant.

During the morning appointments, if I thought I was going to recommend a child for surgery, I frequently would call in another speech pathologist and ask her or him to hear the child's speech and tell me what they heard–so that, later in the day, I would be giving not just one speech pathologist's opinion, but a consensus opinion of at least two.

A few parents would be fearful of surgery, but mostly they were passive and very grateful, seeming to think that the doctors knew best. I never saw the doctors disagree among themselves as to the proper course of action. I also rarely ever saw any really severe and completely unrepaired cleft palate cases. In those cases, the first surgery would have been done within days of birth–the need would have been that clear and apparent.

The degree of cosmetic disfigurement, in severe cleft-lip/cleft-palate situations, is so extreme that, in some cases, the mother–who may have begun to bond with her baby in spite of the disfigurement–reported feeling that she had to begin bonding or connecting with her baby all over again, after the initial cosmetic surgery, because the baby's appearance was so dramatically different that it seemed like a different baby! Dramatically better looking, yes, but also quite dramatically *different*!

A GIRL'S LIFE IN THE CITY

In my hours away from work, whenever I met a guy and he asked me what I did, I would say that I worked at Walter Reed Army Medical Center. Almost invariably, he would say, "Oh, you're a nurse!" Then, I would usually say, "No, I'm a neurosurgeon!" I would savor his confusion and discomfort for a few seconds, before letting him off the hook by admitting that I was actually a speech-language pathologist, and then, probably, having to explain what that was.

Bridge

I learned to play bridge in college, but I played a lot of it when I was at Walter Reed. Through bridge, I met several friends whom I cherish to this day. I knew Anita Ross through the Rehabilitation Group at Walter Reed, and Anita said to me one day, "Do you play bridge?" That's when my social life in our nation's capital really began. Anita worked with Peggy Borsay in Education and Training at Walter Reed, so Peggy came into our new bridge group. Anita's roommate, Pat Plunkert, joined, and she brought in Richard Brawley, who worked with Pat at the U.S. Geological Survey, and so on.

I had many exciting, humorous, even crazy times with various combinations of those friends. For example: one time, returning with Richard to his apartment, after an afternoon of swimming, we were alarmed to see fire trucks in front of his building. Hurrying upstairs through the smoke, we were surprised to find a fireman standing in his boots near Richard's oven, holding up a charred remnant and saying, "Your *chick*-en is done!"

Crochet

I think it was before one of my trips, that I discovered crochet. I thought that I would like to have something to do on the airplane. I had tried knitting, and I didn't like it, and I never enjoyed the hard work of reading (to this day I believe I am an undiagnosed dyslexic). I was at the main hospital by myself while the rest of my section was still located at the Forest Glen Annex, a few miles away–so I was a bit isolated from my professional peers. But the Red Cross office was just around the corner from mine. When I was talking to one of the Red Cross women, she said, "Why don't you try crochet?" I said that I would, but I didn't know how. She said that she would teach me.

She did teach me, and it went very fast–even though I am left-handed, and she was right-handed. After that I made afghans, mostly baby afghans. I made a couple of sweaters, including a purple popcorn-stitch sweater that I wore on my first date with David and that David remembers to this day.

Nowadays, I'm still making afghans, and I usually have a couple already made and stored in a drawer–an inventory ready for any situation. Nevertheless, when I hear that a relative or friend is pregnant, I will start and finish a specific afghan, for that specific baby, well before the baby arrives!

Travels Abroad

The summer I graduated from high school, I was invited to accompany a couple of my classmates, Beverly and Judy, on a trip to Europe. Beverly planned to pick up a Volkswagen "Beetle" automobile in

Brussels, drive it around Europe, and then ship it back to Chicago just before we returned by air.

When I talked to my parents about the trip, in prospect, I said, "I don't think I'm ready to go to Europe. I don't know enough about Europe yet." My father said, "Go to Europe! You will learn about it from being there and seeing it." So that was my first significant trip outside the United States. We three girls traveled through England, Italy, France, Germany, Austria, Belgium, and Holland.

All told, we traveled through Europe for a total of about six weeks! Right out of high school! My father was *so* right; I learned a *lot* about Europe, and it certainly inspired my appetite for more travel when I was older. Of course, my parents supplied the money for my first "Grand Tour" of The Continent.

Did I mention that I had the best parents on the planet?

We managed to get around all right, even though none of us spoke much of any European language. My most vivid memory about getting along in Italian was when Beverly and I went to an Italian bakery, in Venice, to get a cake for Judy's birthday. We didn't speak any Italian; they didn't speak any English. We tried every form of pantomime, struggling to mime the blowing out of candles, etc. They had no idea what we wanted. Finally, I just broke out singing, "Happy Birthday To You," and Beverly joined in. Apparently, the little birthday ditty had already gone viral, worldwide, because *that* they understood, and we got a very nice birthday cake to celebrate Judy's birthday.

103

It's interesting that my husband had a very similar experience years later when we were traveling in Spain. I sent him out to a grocery/butcher shop in Madrid to get the makings for sandwiches—for lunches on our trip the next day, in a rental car, to the Costa Del Sol.

David had only his high school Spanish—which provided him a little more vocabulary than my vocabulary in Italian—but he didn't know the words for "sliced turkey," and the butchers knew no English at all. Finally, after several attempts, David's solution was quite similar to mine in Italy. He simply started making gobbling sounds like a turkey, and somehow—from David's quick motions with his hand—the butcher got the idea and supplied the word for "sliced," which was "lancet" or perhaps "lan-ced" Whatever the word for "turkey" turned out to be, David added the word "lancet" to his Spanish vocabulary and he came home with all the makings of turkey sandwiches for our trip.

The trip with Judy and Beverly was my first trip out of the United States—and my last until I was out of college and graduate school and working in Washington, D.C. But when I started traveling again, I tried my best to make the most of it.

My African Safari

"Pam, let's go to Africa!"

I met Sue Warek at a party, at a friend's home, and we talked about going to Africa. We found that we both had always wanted to see Africa. After a while, she said "Would you go on a safari with me?"

"Why not?"

Besides wanting to see Africa, we had just one thing in common: we were both handicapped. Sue had a significant spinal deformity, but she got around fine, and the trip worked out. We both managed with our handicaps very well.

Once we made our reservations, it turned out that our safari trip would be for three weeks—so I knew I had to pack a lot of stuff. The air flight was really long; I remember having to get up often, to walk the aisle, so I wouldn't get cramps in my legs. It was a charter trip, so it was all one flight. Wow! It seemed to take forever!

When I first got off the plane in Kenya, I looked around and I thought, "I can see; I don't need my glasses here!" I'd never been where the air was so clean before. I could see for miles. Maybe I took the air in Washington, D.C. for granted. Was it dirtier, or just full of more water vapor? I don't know. Never before or since have I seen such clean, transparent air as in Kenya!

We were scheduled to see Kenya, Tanzania, and Ethiopia. When we landed in Nairobi, we were met by the tour guides, and we drove in a bus to Kenya's Amboseli National Park. We camped in tents there, in a "tent hotel." Tents for dining. Tents for sleeping. There were even toilets in the sleeping tents, set apart by a curtain.

Someone told us, "You may hear some monkeys tonight, jumping around on top of your tents." I thought, *If the monkeys can jump on the tents, can the lions be far behind?* Sure enough—I remember that first night—hearing the lions roaring. I didn't get much sleep that night!

105

In the morning, after a hearty breakfast, we got started. Every day, we would get into land rovers and would travel around, looking for animals. One day we saw 17 elephants: mamas, babies, big daddies, and we saw a lion nursery of 3 mamas and 15-16 baby lions playing around.

We stayed in a different hotel every night. The first night was the only tent-hotel. Every other night, we stayed in luxurious regular hotels. We saw wildebeest and rhinoceros. One day we saw two hippos in a fight, near a water hole—two bulls fighting over the nearby cows, I suppose. At a shallow river, we watched for some time. We saw a lion eating a zebra, and I thought, *now I understand survival of the fittest, better than ever before.* We saw a leopard, just sitting in a tree. It was the only leopard we saw. They told us that seeing any leopard at all was pretty rare.

We stayed once in a treetop resort—a plush resort high up in the trees—like tree-houses. At that location, they had lights that lit up a lake at night. Animals would come to the water to drink at night, in the lights. Once, we saw a type of antelope called a "bongo." [32]

Toward the end of the trip I got sick—nauseous, not feeling well. I got better—but Sue came down with pneumonia and was admitted to hospital—so we didn't go to Ethiopia; I stayed with her in Kenya. After the

[32] Wikipedia.com tells us that the Bongo is among the largest of the African forest antelope species.... "Bongos are characterized by a striking reddish-brown coat, black and white markings, white-yellow stripes and long slightly spiraled horns. Indeed, bongos are the only "tragelaphid" in which both sexes have horns. Wikipedia tells us also that the genus *Tragelaphus* contains several species of bovine, all of which are relatively antelope-like.

group returned from Ethiopia, we were supposed to fly home–on a charter flight that was included in our pre-paid tour package. If we missed that flight, we would have to buy tickets on a later, scheduled flight, and we would have to pay about another $400 each.

The doctor said, "Don't tell the chartered-flight people that she has pneumonia, because the pilot can put you off the plane, refusing to fly until you get off the plane. But –once in the air–ask for her to get oxygen. She'll need it!"

Well, we got onto the plane, and before takeoff Sue was wheezing with every breath.

UHHH–HUHHH!.................
UHHH–HUHHH!....................... UHHH–HUHHH.

I said, "You have to try to look happy, so they won't know you're sick. She started grinning like a Jack-O-Lantern, as she wheezed and wheezed. It was hysterical! She kept saying, "I know I'm going to die now–but I can die happy, because I've seen Africa! I know I'm going to die, but ... I've seen Africa!"

While she wheezed and wheezed, I just kept thinking, *Oh my God–she's going to die! And how am I going to explain to her mother that I killed her daughter, because I was too cheap to wait for her to get better and buy another airplane ticket?*

Well, the plane wasn't 3 inches off the ground before I hollered, "SHE NEEDS OXYGEN!" The flight attendant–they were "stewardesses" then–came right away, and she said, What's the trouble?

"SHE NEEDS OXYGEN!"

"Are you her doctor?"

Oh God, they know I'm not a doctor; they probably won't supply oxygen without a prescription or a doctor's say-so. Suddenly, I was struck with terror.

"No, but I work in a hospital."

"Are you her nurse?"

"No, but I work in a hospital. She needs oxygen!"

(Pause)

"Well...How much oxygen does she need?"

Uh, Oh! I thought. *The gig is up! How much oxygen does she need???* I didn't know anything about ordering oxygen. (I'm just a speech pathologist.) *Does it come in GRAMS or MILLIMETERS? NANOHERTZ or MEGAGLOBS?*

I swallowed hard, twice, and I offered, "Oh...about medium."

The attendant disappeared, and I started to worry: *She knows I don't have a clue! She's going up to tell the pilot, who'll turn the plane around and radio for an emergency landing—BACK AT NAIROBI! NINE THOUSAND MILES FROM HOME!*

In about a minute, the attendant returned, carrying an oxygen machine, with a hose and mask. And, believe it or not—on the machine, there was a valve, labeled in big letters: HIGH, LOW, and *MEDIUM!*

I was dumbfounded. I'm not a Catholic, but if ever I wished for a rosary, or some powerful prayer aid, it was then. I fervently wanted to thank God—wherever She was—for my reprieve.

Once Sue got the oxygen, she recovered so much that the attendants decided she was just nervous about flying; they didn't imagine anything about pneumonia. So then, the copilot comes back to check on her, and he invites her up to the cockpit. She gets up there and is chatting away with the pilots—and I have to stay back in steerage! For at least an hour!

Eventually, just before lunch, she returned, and it was all, "Oh, it was so much fun to be up there with the pilots. I could see out the windshield, and they told me all about all the levers and dials and stuff.... That copilot is so-o nice!"

All of a sudden, against all of my personal principles—and despite my so-recent spiritual re-awakening—I wanted to shut off her oxygen!

After we got back, we didn't keep in very good touch. A few years later, I heard that she had died.

Not from pneumonia, I hope.

My Trip To Copenhagen

My friend Connie Laws, head of Welfare and Recreation, said that the travel agent that we worked with had tickets to Copenhagen. I said, "When? How much?"

"In about a week. I don't know the price."

I called the travel agent and asked how much the tickets were. He said, "This includes the round-trip airfare, hotel lodging and breakfast every day. The cost is $185 for everything."

"How many tickets do you have."

"Ten."

"I'll take them all!"

I knew that I could find ten people—at that incredible price—to take the trip. So I just started calling all of my friends, including my friend Pat Plunkert. Pat and I had planned that weekend to go to the beach, at Rehoboth, Delaware.

I said to Pat, "Pat, we're not going to Rehoboth this weekend!

"Oh! Where are we going?"

"We're going to Copenhagen."

As calm as could be, she said, "Oh—O.K."

I called another great friend, Richard Brawley, and he said, "I'm in." I called Mary Hamilton, who joined in with her friend (later her husband) John Modderman. In the end, I had no trouble at all rounding up nine people (plus me) to take this fabulous trip, for just $185.

I remember that the agent had said, "For heavens sake, don't tell anybody on the trip how much you paid for these tickets." I instructed all of our group, that they were not to even discuss it among themselves. On the airplane, others were saying things like, "Isn't this a wonderful trip, we only paid $1400 dollars," or whatever.

It was a grand trip. In Copenhagen we split up into groups. Richard and I were crazy about Royal Copenhagen dinnerware. We went to the Royal Copenhagen store or outlet, where he bought a whole service of Royal Copenhagen. He and I walked back and forth between Royal Copenhagen and another store so many times, with Pat in tow, that finally Pat said,

"Look—I'm going to sit right here on this bench. You and Richard go back and forth as many times as you want, and when you are finished, I'll be right here!"

We rented a car and did a lot of driving. At a gas station, Richard couldn't get the hose nozzle loose from the gas pump. He cursed and swore. Finally, Pat got out and just lifted it off for him. Then he *really* swore!

Another time, we were at Elsinore Castle—the castle in which Shakespeare's *Hamlet* is set—and Richard couldn't get our little European car into reverse so he could back out of a parking space. I don't know how that was finally solved, but we're not still there, so someone must have figured it out! (Probably, Pat.)

On another occasion, when I was driving, we approached from a two-lane highway to meet and cross a four-lane highway. Stopping, before making a left turn onto the busier thoroughfare, I said to Pat, who was sitting next to me, "Tell me when it's O.K. to turn." Pat replied, "O.K." So I quickly accelerated and turned out across two lanes of traffic coming from my left, into the nearest lane of traffic coming from my right on the crossing highway—and my passengers practically lost their dinners. Richard dived for the floor, in the back seat, and Pat said—I don't remember what she said—but she clearly had *meant*, "O.K.—I'll tell you when it's clear," *not*, "O.K.—It's clear *now!*"

Ever since, we have been much more careful with our words in such situations.

We went to the Tivoli Gardens: a compact theme park in Copenhagen. Tivoli was a wonderful park that the entire group enjoyed. I wondered if Walt

Disney had once seen Tivoli and taken his inspiration for Disneyland/Disney World from it.[33]

Athens, The Greek Islands, Egypt

Greek national hero Spyros Moustaklis—an officer in the 20th Century Greek Army—was tortured and brain-damaged by the Greek Military Junta during the Time Of The Junta (1967–74).[34] He is variously

---

[33] Tivoli Gardens (or simply **Tivoli**) is a famous amusement park and pleasure garden in Copenhagen, Denmark. The park opened on 15 August 1843 and is the second-oldest operating amusement park in the world. Walt Disney, during a trip overseas with his wife Lilly, visited Tivoli Gardens. Walt was so impressed with Tivoli that he immediately decided Disneyland should try to emulate its "happy and unbuttoned air of relaxed fun." Disney said of his Tivoli-inspired theme park, "Disneyland will never be completed. It will continue to grow as long as there is imagination left in the world"—echoing a sentiment by Tivoli's Georg Carstensen, over a century earlier in 1844, who said, "Tivoli will never, so to speak, be finished." —Wikipedia.com, retrieved May 1, 2016.

[34] "Major **Spyros Moustaklis** (Greek: Σπύρος Μουστακλής; Missolonghi, 1926-1986) was an officer of the Greek Army. During the military junta years in Greece, he actively opposed the dictatorship and suffered permanent damage as the result of torture, making him a symbol of the anti-junta resistance.

"A graduate of the Hellenic Military Academy, Moustaklis was one of the few Army officers that took part in the attempted Navy revolt in 1973 against the Papadopoulos junta. After the revolt was betrayed and suppressed, he was arrested and tortured by the Greek Military Police in the torture chambers of EAT/ESA. He was arrested on 22 May 1973 and stayed at the EAT/ESA torture centre for 47 days, but despite the efforts of his interrogators, he did not betray his colleagues. During a torture session he suffered brain trauma after a violent blow to his carotid artery and was subsequently rushed to hospital in a vegetative state. His life was saved, but he was left paralyzed for the rest of his life. Only

recorded as holding the ranks of major, colonel, and (in disability retirement and/or posthumously) the honorary rank of Lt. General. I knew him as "Col. Moustaklis."

I originally understood that the main damage from the torture was from electrical shock, though I have since learned that he suffered a massive stroke–caused by a tremendous blow to the neck, which pounded his carotid artery so hard that a heavy wave of blood pressure traveled up to his brain and burst a vessel.

After the Junta was overthrown in 1974, the U.S. Embassy in Athens requested the State Department to arrange an evaluation of Moustaklis by the Walter Reed Army Medical Center. After persistent urging from Athens, Washington agreed, and Colonel Moustaklis was brought to Walter Reed.

"Would you work with him?," I was asked. "As long as he understands and speaks some English," I said. "Otherwise I will have trouble."

Moustaklis had spoken some English–when he had previously been able to speak. So I got the referral to see him.

I saw the Colonel twice a week; his wife came with him every time. She was very sweet, very grateful, and she was able to interpret my English to the Colonel, and his limited Greek expressions to me. He didn't have

following physiotherapy and rehabilitation for five months he was able to regain limited movement."

–https://en.wikipedia.org/wiki/Spyros_Moustaklis   Retrieved April 25, 2016.

much speech or language. We did a little singing and a few conversational things. He needed to be able to communicate his basic needs of living–no reading or writing was entertained. He did make some progress, no question about it. I saw him for maybe 4 or 5 weeks. Walter Reed gave instructions for the types of continuing therapy he should have. Then we prepared to discharge him.

On the day of the Colonel's discharge, Mrs. Moustaklis said to me, "You must come to Greece and visit me. I really want to have you come visit us in Athens! Please tell me you'll come!"

I said, "You shouldn't invite me, unless you are really serious. I'm single; I have no family responsibilities. I will come!"

She said "*Please* come."

"OK I will come. Could I bring a friend with me? My friend Mary is an occupational therapist. She may be able, now that Colonel Moustaklis is out of the hospital, to help him further by giving him some ideas about functioning with his handicaps in daily living. That is what an O.T. does."

"Certainly! Bring your friend!"

I said, "I will come!"

So I invited my friend Mary to come with me. Mary said, "Great! I'll be glad to do it."

After returning to Greece, Mrs. Moustaklis commented publicly about her husband's visit to Walter Reed, as follows (quoted from a U.S. diplomatic cable):

1. WIFE OF SPYROS MOUSTAKLIS, RETIRED COLONEL HELLENIC ARMY, EXPRESSED APPRECIATION TO EMBASSY JANUARY 29 RE EMBASSY-ARRANGED WALTER REED VISIT. MRS. MOUSTAKLIS SAID HER HUSBAND HAS MADE SOME PROGRESS, HIS SPEECH HAS IMPROVED, AND MORALE-WISE HE FEELS BETTER. COLONEL AND MRS. MOUSTAKLIS GRATEFUL FOR MEDICAL ATTENTION AT WALTER REED HOSPITAL AND FOR INSTRUCTIONS RECEIVED FOR FURTHER REHABILITATION EFFORTS.

2. MOUSTAKLIS AND WIFE MET WITH ATHENS PRESS FOLLOWING ARRIVAL JANUARY 28 AND STATED MEDICAL CARE RECEIVED IN U.S. SURPASSED EXPECTATIONS. MRS. MOUSTAKLIS SAID U.S. PRESS REPORTED HER HUSBAND'S CASE AND SHE WAS APPRECIATIVE OF ASSISTANCE OFFERED BY SENATOR KENNEDY, REP. ROSENTHAL AND HFAC [House Foreign Affairs Committee] COUNSEL HACKETT (NO MENTION MADE OF EMBASSY'S ASSISTANCE). MRS. MOUSTAKLIS ADDED THAT AMERICAN PHYSICIANS WERE OPTIMISTIC THAT HER HUSBAND WOULD IMPROVE GRADUALLY THROUGH LONG TERM THERAPY. ATHENS NEWSPAPERS REPORTED PROMINENTLY MOUSTAKLIS SATISFACTION

[35] Public Library of US Diplomacy. HOSPITALIZATION FOR COLONEL MOUSTAKLIS. Jan. 30, 1975.
−https://wikileaks.org/plusd/cables/1975ATHENS00833_b.html. Retrieved Feb. 3, 2015.

WITH U.S. TRIP, NATIONAL TV CARRIED SPOT
INTERVIEW.

Within six months, I and my friend Mary traveled to Athens, Greece. Colonel Moustaklis was then in a residential facility in Greece, working on his speech and motor-neural problem.

Mrs. Moustaklis had us to dinner at her apartment. She served us what I thought was a fabulously impressive dinner of lobster. I was feeling quite satisfied, when she then said, "Now for the main course"–and the maid then brought out a leg of lamb, with all the trimmings!

On that visit to her apartment, she said, "Oh, I wish you were living here, because there is a girl with cerebral palsy, who needs help." Of course, Mary and I went right down to the girl's apartment to help her, and Mary showed her mother how to help her become more independent in activities of daily living.

After seeing Colonel and Mrs. Moustaklis in Athens, we took a cruise to see the Greek islands, etc. We had never been to Greece before, so we decided to see as much of it as we could. As far as I'm concerned, it was absolutely one of the very best trips or tours I ever took in my whole life.

There were a lot of single men working on the ship, so that was a lot of fun. There was a costume ball on the ship, and I really wanted to participate. So Mary and I worked out a costume plan for both of us.

She said, "I'll go as a bottle of champagne."

I said, "What will I go as–the bubbles?"

"Oh that's a good idea."

Mary asked the bartenders on the ship to save all their corks from the bottles of wine they had opened. We used straight pins to attach them to a cylinder of cardboard, forming the body of a cork-shaped hat (with the pins pointing outward from Mary's head, of course)! I then surrounded Mary with two more large pieces of poster board, with the word "*Champagne*" lettered onto them.

Dressed in all black, I attached blown up balloons to my black turtle-neck. I had to be sure to keep a reasonable distance from Mary and her prickly cork-hat. We connected the two of us with ribbons passing from Mary's costume to me, representing the bubbles streaming from behind the cork! When we went to leave the cabin and go to the ball, I was so wide I could not get through the door. I had to remove a lot of the balloons, and put them back on once I got through the door.

Getting around the ship with balloons all around me—and keeping a good distance from Mary so as to not to pop all the balloons—was a challenge, but we eventually made it to the main ballroom for the costume contest.

The ballroom was so crowded that there were no chairs available by the time we got there, so I just crouched down on the floor with the "bubbles" surrounding and completely covering me. Along came a waitress, carrying a huge tray of drinks, filled with a Greek liqueur called Uzo. To her, I merely looked like a pile of balloons. Suddenly, I moved or straightened up, and she was so startled that she upset the drinks and immediately I had the drinks all over me. As the cold liquid was running down my back, all I could think about was that I was going to smell like Uzo for the rest of my life!

Despite everything, we were awarded second place for our joint costume.

There was one guy on the ship that I was attracted to, from the moment I met him. He was traveling with his mother. Once at the end of a day ashore, he and his mother were at the top of the gangplank when we came back to the ship. I saw them together and immediately tripped and fell down onto the gangplank. But I was down and up like lightning, because I was trying to impress this man, and I was so embarrassed. His mother said, "I've never seen anyone fall and get up so fast."

One evening he asked me to dance, and Mary was terrified because he was swinging me around and throwing me up in the air. A lot of people gave us space on the dance floor, because he was really quite the dancer. It's a wonder he didn't finish the job of breaking my back in two! (My back, of course had always been structurally weak because of the Spina Bifida condition with which I was born.)

The cruise covered the islands of Crete and Rhodes, also Santorini and Mykonos– the two islands that were the most Greek and the most unlike any place I had ever seen.

We saw so many very attractive Greek men that we kept nudging each other and calling each other's attention to them. We had to come up with a code word to speak, every time we wanted the other to take note of another hunk coming into view! We chose the word "sidewalk"–who knows why, maybe we were just walking on a sidewalk when we thought of it. Anyway, for awhile we were saying the word "sidewalk" a lot!

Because there was some trouble between Greece and Turkey at the time, our ship was diverted from Turkey to Egypt. Wow! That could not have been better! My parents had been to Egypt, and I desperately wanted to go.

We rode camels from the Sphinx to the Pyramids. At the Pyramids, the guides were saying, "Don't go into the Pyramid if you have back trouble, asthma, claustrophobia, etc., etc. I said, "I'll meet you out here." Mary said, "Pam Silverwood, we will never be here again; this is the chance of a lifetime! You get into that Pyramid." I had *never* known Mary to be so stern!

You had to bend down really low because the ceilings of the passageway were so low–but I made it and I ultimately made it all the way in to the tomb chamber of the Great Pyramid of Cheops.

The King's (tomb) Chamber was a room 34 by 17 feet and very interesting. I was glad I went inside. Later, we went to the Museum of Egyptian Antiquities, in Cairo, and saw King Tut's mask of gold, and many other items that simply took your breath away.

Of course we wanted to do some shopping while in Egypt. We found a store that had lovely caftans but they refused to take our traveler's checks–so Mary went in a cab to a bank to cash some checks and then rushed back to the store. She later told me she feared for her life in that cab ride. She got back none too soon, as I was getting vibes from the shop owners that did not make me feel safe. When she got back, the shop owner wanted to change the price on the caftans, but Mary said, "NO, this is what you told us and this is what we are paying and that's all." She picked up the package and paid the man and we both were very glad to get out of that area safe and sound.

Later, back home, there was an exhibit of artifacts from King Tut's tomb at the National Gallery of Art, in Washington D.C. I went to see it with Richard and Pat. We waited nine hours in line, but we finally got to see it all; so many precious gems and gold artifacts that were buried with him! Amazing.

To me, Egypt had been so different from any country I had ever been to, so totally different, and I thought the art things were so unusual. Everything was fascinating to me in Egypt. After the trip, I made a huge needlepoint picture of an Egyptian scene. It took me months and months to complete. After my marriage, David insisted that we spend the money to have that needlepoint work professionally framed. It hangs on our wall to this day!

Years later, I went to Greece again, this time with David and our son Andrew—who was then nineteen. I had long since lost touch with Mrs. Moustaklis, and no longer had her contact information. But, on the way in from the airport, I happened to ask the cab driver whether he had ever heard of Spyros Moustaklis.

"Oh, of course!" he said immediately. "Everybody knows about Spyros Moustaklis! He's a national hero!" At our hotel, he used the desk clerk's phone to call Directory Assistance and get Mrs. Moustaklis' phone number—but she was not in. So, he took the number with him and called us, later that evening, to say that he'd reached her, and that she wanted very much to see us.

She met us at a restaurant we chose—but letting *us* entertain *her* at *that venue* was not what she had in mind. She took us to another restaurant, as her guests—an elegant restaurant—with lunch served on a huge outdoor terrace dominated by the nearby Acropolis and the iconic Temple of Athena (The Parthenon) overlooking us from above.

Later she took us to another site, where she showed us a monument that had been erected in honor and memory of her late husband, in recognition of his contribution to the struggle for democracy in Greece. He had also been awarded the honorary rank of Lieutenant General, and his name was given to the camp that housed the Recruit Training Centre in his home town.[36]

Asia

My last trip abroad as a single girl was to Hong Kong and Thailand, with my friend Peggy Borsay. In Thailand, I bought a set of eight place settings of dining utensils, in bronze ware. In Hong Kong, we just shopped and shopped, including my having a silk outfit made for me by a Chinese tailor. At the prices charged in those days, when the value of the dollar was still riding high, I couldn't help remembering one of my father's teasing jibes: "You're losing money every minute you're not buying one!" In any case, it was one of the most economical garments I ever bought—except

[36]   —https://en.wikipedia.org/wiki/Spyros_Moustaklis. Retrieved April 20, 2016.

the truth is, I really didn't wear it much once I got it home.

When we returned to the States, at Hawaii, I was detained in customs because I couldn't find all my receipts of purchase. I was scared to death, but I finally found them all and was allowed to return into the United States without paying an arbitrary import duty.

THRIFT

When I was about 12, I once heard my mother and father talking downstairs. I heard my father say, "I don't know where our next meal is coming from."

When I was grown up and discussed this with Mom as an adult, my ever-practical mother said, "Well, we could always have just sold a building." At that time, my parents were only "real-estate poor"—sometimes described as "cash-poor" or having a "cash-flow problem." My father had invested in several rental buildings over the years. Though the mortgage balances were being paid down, and the buildings were appreciating, the mortgage payments didn't leave much cash available, from the rental income, to apply to our comfortable life style. When my father expressed his financial worry to my mother, they simply didn't happen to have a whole lot of ready cash in the bank.

My mother was the most adaptable person I ever knew. But what my father said then really stayed with me. Although I am not a hoarder, all my life, ever since, I have needed to keep my cupboards *well stocked!* Shortly after I met my husband, David, when I was 40, he was surprised and amused one day when he discovered that the washer/dryer in my tiny kitchen was filled with staple foods!

To this day, I don't leave in the car for an afternoon's trip, without taking an apple or a Coke with me. David and I joke about my fear of "starving to death," but being hungry without being able to do something about it is a very real concern for me—as real as needing to have some idea where I will find the next rest room on the road! (Of course, the reader will recall my anxiety in high school about the threat of an "accident," arising from my very limited control of my bladder. We did not then have the array of commercial incontinence products that we have today.)

When we adopted our son, until he started third grade I clothed him entirely– except for shoes–with hand-me-downs and purchases from thrift stores and yard sales, and he *never* looked as if he were wearing second-hand clothes. It is simply amazing, the quality of clothing you can find in thrift stores, if you look carefully–especially in a high-income area such as Washington, D.C. and its suburbs.

Kids grow so fast, it's crazy to buy all new clothing every time they explode to the next size.

I have long been thankful to my friend Mary for first introducing me to the idea of patronizing thrift stores. My family was quite financially comfortable during my formative years. So there was nothing is my upbringing that so much as suggested that thrift stores were something to consider. When Mary first spoke to me about thrift stores, I was quite taken aback. *My father was a very successful real estate professional; why would I ever need to go to a thrift store?* But after my initial hesitation, and after once visiting such a store and seeing the possibilities, I was definitely converted to a new way of seeing things.

David once went to a thrift store to find a blue blazer to take on a cruise–a garment cheap enough to throw away, after the last "formal" night on the ship, rather than lug an extra garment all around Europe. For $3.75 he found–in his exact size–a Botany 500 blue blazer that appeared in every respect brand-new and was better in every way than the one he had planned to keep! David still has the Botany 500 in his closet, and expects to keep that classic garment for the rest of his life.

Mary also was not shy about scavenging things she might have seen sitting out on a curb for disposal. She is quite clever and handy with tools, and one time, when we were single girls, she made an extension leaf for my dining room table, from an old board that she acquired somewhere. So Mary convinced me that it was not shameful to scavenge perfectly good things or materials that others were throwing away.

I did not become the scavenger that Mary was, but after David and I had Andrew to raise, I involved David into scavenging an old refrigerator box. Previously, we had acquired a refrigerator box somehow—maybe from a furniture store—from which we carved windows and a door to make a playhouse for Andrew, when he was small.

That playhouse didn't last a long time, being just a cardboard box, after all, and being subject to hard play. Some time later, driving home from work, I saw another refrigerator box sitting on a curb. I knew that my little car would not accommodate a large refrigerator box, but when David came home from work I sent him after it with our minivan. He was gone about 20 minutes, and when he returned I asked him, "Did you find it?"

"Yep, I found it," he replied.

"So you've got it then?"

"Nope, I don't have it. I couldn't bring it home."

"Wouldn't fit in the van, I suppose?"

"That's not exactly the problem."

"What then?"

"There's a refrigerator in it!"

When my mother was alive, she would often compliment me on some article of clothing or costume jewelry and ask me where I had purchased it. I would usually chirp, happily, "From a thrift store." My mother was always amazed. She had not only grown up with a fair amount of wealth, but once Dad got established—even through The Depression—she had always been very comfortable. Though Mom had been a volunteer worker in charitable thrift stores, in both Chicago and Florida, she never in her life thought to *patronize* a thrift store—charitable or otherwise—herself. She was also not proficient at hunting up things on sale; she had always had plenty. At age 75—when David and I were about to get married— she still hadn't changed her shopping habits.

However, as she aged further toward an eventual 103, there was a time or two when I found some blouse or scarf that I thought was perfect for her. I would say, "Now Mom, I have to tell you that I found this at a thrift store, but I think it's perfect for you. If you don't want it, I'll just wear it myself. What do you think?" I never had to take a single thing back and put it in my own closet. Faced with a garment as good as new, one that suited her to a "T," she was able to adjust.

Adjust! My heavens yes! My mother was the most adjustable, adaptable person ever!

"THERE HE IS !"

One Friday afternoon at work, when I was still single, I got a call from my friend, Joanne Schwartz.

"Let's go to a Singles Discussion tonight, at the Rockville Unitarian Church. There should be some new men there!"

"Oh, Joanne—don't you get it? I am *not* going to find Prince Charming, at my age." (I'm thinking, *Besides—I walk funny!*) I *say*, "Besides, I am too worn out; this has been the week from Hell! I'll watch a movie with you, though. Let's just relax into a good Cary Grant flick!" Well, Joanne is nothing if not persistent. "Look," she says, "even if we don't meet anyone, there's a good chance we'll have an interesting discussion."

So before long, I was walking with Joanne into a Rockville Unitarian Church classroom. Just before the discussion started, in came a guy I'd never seen before. He was blond with a sandy beard, tall enough, in a red cashmere sweater.

There he is! I thought. I was immediately smitten.

The discussion that night was, "How Do You Let Someone Of The Opposite Sex Know Of Your Interest In Him/Her?" All I remember is that I was saying something aloud about... what *was* I saying, anyway?

David (he was wearing a name tag) responded with, "Pam—I know exactly how you feel."

He *knows* how I *feel* (swoon)!!! That was it.

After the discussion was over, I drifted over to the social hall, hoping to see him again, but I guess I was a little late. It seems that David had entered the social hall, where he spotted someone who raised a painful memory, and he decided to go.

On my way toward the social hall, I caught sight of him crossing over into the cloakroom. I quickly positioned myself in the doorway he would have to pass through on his way out. He emerged from the cloakroom in a Burberry topcoat. *Here he comes! Look Good!*

"Good night, Pam," he said warmly." And he was gone!

"Damn!

There were several other guys there, and I talked with some of them, but I couldn't stop thinking about the one who got away. I didn't know it then, but David, at nearly 40, was still quite self-protective as regards women—a little slow to make (*but very slow to break*) a commitment.

So I commiserated with myself:

I'll never forgive Joanne for dragging me out here tonight!

What was I thinking?!

Won't I ever learn?!

OHH!!!

The next morning was Saturday, and Joanne was at my apartment, reading over the ads for church bazaars. It was December first—Christmas bazaar season.

"Look, Pam! 'The River Road Church Holiday Bazaar! That's David's church! He said he goes to the River Road Unitarian Church!"

The rest is history.

And that is why we call Joanne our Fairy Godmother!

Tomo-San Takahashi

Shortly after we moved into our house, I had to leave David alone while I took a business trip. I had volunteered to be a "site visitor"–representing the American Speech and Hearing Association (ASHA)–to evaluate the eligibility of specific hospitals for the renewal of accreditation for their speech pathology programs. So I traveled to New York to review a particular program.

When I returned Friday night, instead of David picking me up at the airport, as planned, I was surprised to see my good friend, Pat Plunkert, approaching me.

"Hi," she said.

"Why are you here," I asked. "Where's David."

"David asked me to pick you up."

"Why?" I asked again.

"Well, he had a little accident."

"Accident? What kind of accident," I asked, choking back my terror.

"Well, actually, he's in the hospital."

"HOSPITAL? Is he OK?"

"Yes, He's OK."

This is what happened while I was away: The night before I left, a driver had approached the end of our street, too fast. Although the end of the street was clearly marked with red reflective signs–the lay of the land was such that, in the dark, by automobile headlights, one could mistake a part of our lawn as an offset extension of the street. The driver had driven right onto the part of our lawn that stretches downhill, toward the creek, and become stuck in the "mud"–the earth under the grass, softened by spring rains.

The next afternoon–with me gone to New York–the car was still there mired in the lawn when David returned from work. Soon after he got home, there was a ring of the doorbell, which David answered to find a policeman standing on the front porch, inquiring about the car on the lawn–whether David knew anything about it.

As David stood there with the door partly open, talking with the officer, my cat–Tomo-San Takahashi by name–slipped through the crack to investigate the great outdoors.

Tomo[37] had always been an "indoor" cat. I had never allowed him outside my apartment or–after we bought the house and joined our households–outside the house. I knew nothing of outdoor cats, and David–having been raised on a farm–knew nothing of indoor cats. We had been in the house only about two weeks, and David was having some trouble remembering about keeping Tomo confined–a skill I had long ago honed to perfection.

So, now, the cat is outside, and David is responsible. That is (he fears) about to *become* responsible for having lost my beloved cat, whom I had raised from a kitten.

---

37 "Tomo: A super cool caring Japanese "BRO" who is the best friend you will ever get. Tomos usually stress out a lot, but are always there for people when they need help."
   –Urbandictionary.com, retrieved March, 2016.

Cats like high places, and Tomo's favorite high place in my condo apartment was atop the back of my favorite chair—my upholstered recliner. He not only liked to perch there—on occasion he would take a running start from the back bedroom, zoom the length of the hallway and through the dining and living rooms to launch himself into the air and land, triumphant, atop his favorite perch—high on the chair-back. When David first witnessed this, he was quite impressed—especially since he was, himself, at that moment, enjoying his repose in that very chair. Surprised, is a better word! But he recovered well—and he came to share, to an extent, my fondness for my amazing animal.

I loved my cat, and Tomo had grown up to tolerate me very well. He would sleep on my bed and, through un-numbered moments of relaxation, I had taught him to "wink!"

Yes, that's right, I taught a tomcat to wink at me, in response to my example—winking at him. You may find this hard to believe, but it is true, and David will attest to it. He says that, indeed, he saw Tomo wink back at me—not once but on two occasions.

**Tomo-San Takahashi, all cat and
part tiger.**

So David was not about to lose his beloved's
beloved cat, certainly not so early in our new
relationship together in our new house. Quickly
bringing his conversation with the policeman to a close,
David began to follow Tomo down the street to retrieve
him. Tomo soon enough walked underneath a parked
car, where David expended considerable time and effort
coaxing him out far enough to pick him up.

Heading back to the house, David now found the front door locked against him. At just about that moment, Tomo began to struggle a bit and David—having little experience with city cats—and no experience at all with a cat wearing a collar—

injudiciously slipped a finger under the collar in an attempt to secure the cat within his grasp. Tomo, feeling the collar tighten around his neck, reacted as any wild animal would to an attack upon its neck—he fought back for his freedom and his life.

So we have a contest of wills—Tomo is not going to go willingly back into the house, and certainly not about to tolerate the tightening encirclement of his neck, while David is not about to lose my cat and—he fears—lose me in the bargain. In no time at all, Tomo sinks his sharp teeth and his hind claws deeply into both of David's hands. Does David drop the cat like a hot potato? No. My husband is nothing if not courageous and determined in the defense of his home and marriage—he holds on!

He held on while the policeman reached into David's pocket for the house keys and opened the front door. David dropped the cat inside and locked the door, then immediately asked the policeman for directions to the nearest emergency room. Remember, we have been in our house for less than two weeks, and David is just beginning to know the neighborhood.

So that's how I happened to be at the hospital, entering David's room around 10:30 on a Friday night, having come directly from the airport after a taxing business trip.

David was in the hospital for two weeks. Cat bites and cat-claw wounds are highly infectious, so the hand surgeon who admitted David to the hospital put him under general anesthesia about six times to "debride" and disinfect the wounds—not to mention constant administration of intravenous antibiotics for the duration.

By the time David came home from the hospital, the trees that had been barely in bud were fully leafed out. Spring seemed almost over, and we began to patch up our tripartite relationship, as David's wounds continued healing.

Tomo was all male—very territorial and jealous of David's relationship with me, his only known mistress or master. He did not take easily to sharing his house and his mistress with—as he must have felt—an interloper. David and Tomo existed in a somewhat uneasy peace for about another six months.

When I first saw David in the hospital and heard his story, my immediate reaction was that Tomo would have to go—be taken away to the animal control shelter to be adopted elsewhere or ... worse. But while David was away for those two weeks, Tomo and I returned to the comfortable relationship we had when I had lived with only feline companionship—and Tomo had lived only with me. I began to think that losing Tomo might not be required.

But, I decided, the days of keeping Tomo as a strictly indoor cat would have to be over. We were suburbanites now, tending a lawn and garden, learning to enjoy the outdoors on our back porch. It was not lost on me that it was my own insistence on keeping Tomo confined that had triggered David's compulsion to reconfine him *at any cost.* I told David that I would have to steel myself to letting Tomo outside some fine day, as we worked outdoors, and trust that he would come to remember "where his home is" and not leave us.

So we did that. One weekend, we let Tomo out–and then watched apprehensively as he familiarized himself with our yard and the things in it. That first day, when we went inside, he soon followed us in through the open door.

The next day, we did the same. Tomo hung around nearby, swatting at insects and stalking the birds–and we gradually began to relax our anxious vigil as to where he was and what he was doing. But at the end of the day, he seemed to be missing.

He remained missing, day after day. As the week went by, we gradually and sadly realized that we would have to adjust to our loss–clearly he was not coming back.

On Saturday night, there was a tremendous thunder storm. We wondered where Tomo was–had he found a new foster home, or was he out somewhere in the woods and the storm?

The next day, Sunday again, there was still no Tomo. We thought about him from time to time, but it seemed clear–whatever his new life was like, it wasn't going to include us. I felt like a mother whose child had grown up and moved away, and then decided to cut ties and disappear; we knew a family in which that had happened.

That night, late, David opened the kitchen door to put out the trash for Monday pickup. There was Tomo, on the side porch, just outside the kitchen door.

He walked right in. David came up the stairs to the bedroom, where I was watching television, to tell me. Before he could finish his sentence, Tomo followed him in and hopped right up on the bed.

What a surprise! He *looked* like he had been through a storm—or a cement mixer! His fur was no longer sleek and smooth, but rumpled and sticking out in clumps and patches. We could only try to imagine where he had been for a week, and what he had been through the previous night, during the storm.

So our uneasy peace resumed, and continued—until my mother and her friend Frances came to visit as houseguests. When we learned that my mother's friend had been threatened—hissed at through bared teeth and virtually driven by Tomo from the guest room—I decided my quandary must end. With many shared tears, David and I transported Tomo to the animal shelter, and I closed that chapter of my formerly single life forever.

Our Wedding Ceremony

We wrote our wedding ceremony ourselves; our minister urged us to write it ourselves. He said that doing so requires a couple to think things through together and agree on what they want their marriage to mean. Their collaboration in the writing of what their ceremony will say would be an important early step toward succeeding in their subsequent life together—making of their marriage what they jointly desired and expected.

The alternative, he seemed to say—having the minister declare *for himself and his tradition* what their marriage would be about—would run a risk that the couple might simply hold on to whatever private and individual fantasies of married life they might assume was the way it always would be for them.

In addition to the words we used to describe the symbolism of our ceremony, we acted out for our friends and family what we thought of our marriage as meaning. We had three candles on the altar.[38] Two candles were lit, symbolizing the life of each of us individually, up to that point. A third candle, in the center, was initially unlit, and at some point in the ceremony we jointly took our individual candles and together lit the central candle—representing the joint life we were undertaking together and the family we hoped to create. However, we left the original two candles burning, to represent the individuality of both persons, which we hoped to preserve rather than obliterate in the course of our marriage. We thought that this ceremony was entirely our own creation.

Years later, we learned that similar symbolism had been becoming increasingly popular for 40 years or more—beginning *before* our own marriage. It seems that some Catholics think of it as an unofficial Catholic tradition, some Protestants think it is an unofficial Protestant tradition, and its true origin seems to be obscure.[39]

---

[38] Our "altar" was also of our own design. At my suggestion, David constructed a group of four plywood boxes–8 x 8 inches in cross-section and from 42 to 54 inches tall. I covered them with white linen. After our wedding, we donated our flexible "altar" to the church, for whatever uses it might have in future ceremonies and services.

[39] —https://en.wikipedia.org/wiki/Unity_candle

At the end of our candle ceremony, I presented a long-stemmed red rose to David's widowed father and David presented one to my widowed mother, as a thank you for the adult child that each of them had raised and given to the marriage beginning that day, and to symbolize the presence in spirit of their own respective partners, who were then missing in body.

There was, of course, some song, some prayer, and a declaration by the minister of our new status as husband and wife; then a recessional, to the theme music from *Chariots of Fire,* to which the audience spontaneously applauded—followed by a lovely indoor/outdoor reception on a gorgeous September 4th, 1982, the 52nd anniversary of my parents' wedding!

We had ordered a very special wedding cake for the occasion. David had not wanted to enact what he considered the silly tradition of the newlyweds stuffing cake into each other's mouth. So we also opted not to have a traditional white, layered cake with a couple of dressed up dolls on top. We had our caterer produce instead a cake they described as particularly delicious. It must have been, because while we were greeting and socializing with our guests and having a bunch of wedding pictures taken, the cake was completely consumed by the assembled party—to the extent that we, the wedding couple, never got a taste of it. Nevertheless, our event—and especially the ceremony—was a great success. We know it was, because both our minister and our friend Ed Yoe—a well-known professional event planner—asked to pass on the written text of our wedding to other couples, for

—http://catholicphilly.com/2012/09/think-tank/catholic-spirituality/whats-with-the-unity-candle-in-a-catholic-wedding/

adaptation to those other couples' future wedding ceremonies!

AND THEN, THERE WAS A FAMILY

David and I were both forty when we met. He had been married once, briefly. I, never. But we both had dreamed since childhood of a time when we would raise and love children of our own. David remembers his drawing, at age 5, a floor plan for the house that he dreamed of having someday, in which he would raise a family–a family he meant to be something his family of origin was not.

I was very leery–with a history of Spina Bifida, and with only one kidney–of *bearing* a child, and I thought very favorably of adoption. Nevertheless, we consulted an OB/GYN doctor about my prospects for carrying a child to term and for our child being healthy – *normal*. After the usual examination, the doc said that, even in view of my age and history, there was no reason we couldn't try. So we returned home to think it over.

I thought, and I thought, and I thought. And what I thought was that, at my age, the chances of bearing a Down Syndrome baby were too great for me to face. Of course I knew that fetuses could be tested *in utero* for many kinds of abnormalities, and that things could be done. As it happens, I was and am strongly "pro-choice." But I knew that, for me personally–if events brought me to a decision about abortion–I could not do that. It would be wrong–*for me*. But I also knew that I would feel very bad about my choice if I chose to have a child at 46 or so, and that child were born with a serious abnormality.

So, in view of all the above, we agreed to let it go.

***

When I was a teenager, I once mused to my mother something about my future, about marriage and family. She said something that stayed with me. She said, "You know, Dear, there are no guarantees in life. You may marry, but you may not. It's probably best to live each day as it comes. You don't want to wish your life away, always waiting for something or someone to come along."

I know that my mother's comment was as loving as ever could be and very wise as well. But it could be taken also as a gentle warning. It could have meant, without putting too fine a point on it, that I might not be *able* to have children. After all, my body was compromised—and not in every respect as beautiful and capable as I (or a man) might desire. Here was I, with a weakened spinal column, no left kidney, my feet unusually shaped and with no effective muscles to allow me to point my toes or stand tippy-toe; weak in the ankles, unable to wear high heels; walking forever *on* my heels, as if on stilts—with an attendant loss of balance that would get worse as I aged. Then there were the unknowns—unknown to me at least: whatever condition, genetic or environmental, might have allowed or caused my Spina Bifida....

***

I had already had a very exciting life, with more years to come, and I surely had a good marriage and a good life together with David. What's more, I had long since, in my thirties—before meeting David—given up on the dream that I was even likely to *marry*.

We let it go.

142

And then, my brother Jim and his wife had their first child—and, at 18 months, David and I agreed to babysit for a day, so Jim and Jean could have a day off. Afterward, on the way home, David said that he had been thinking a lot, lately. He had recently read a story, in the "Personal Business" section of *Business Week,* about adoption.

We both knew the odds were against an older couple getting the proverbial "healthy *infant*" from an agency. But the article in *Business Week* said, in part, that the older couples who find a healthy infant to adopt are those who tell everyone they know that they are *looking* for a baby. We agreed; that is *just* what we would do.

The following Sunday, after church, David approached our minister to tell him about the *Business Week* story and to say that we were telling everyone we knew that we were looking for a baby to adopt. The minister pointed to the rear of the sanctuary and said, "Do you see that couple at the end of the aisle there? They recently adopted. You should talk to them."

At the end of the aisle were a couple just a little younger than ourselves. As we approached, we could see that the man was holding the most beautiful infant we had ever seen. The couple's names were Linda and Ken. They told us they had adopted through a self-help organization called Families for Private Adoption.[40] There would be a monthly meeting of that organization on Wednesday, at a home across the street from the church. Could we come?

Could we!

[40] Families For Private Adoption website: www.ffpa.org/

We attended the Wednesday meeting, where we met a houseful of couples, most of them accompanied by adopted children ranging from newborn to a few years.

During the program, the group's attorney was introduced–Jim Schrybman. At some point, Mr. Schrybman announced, "I'm looking for housing for a birth mother; could anyone help me out with that?"

I saw David's eyes, across the room, meeting mine. We both nodded.

We approached Mr. Schrybman to ask about his birth mother. He said, first off, that this birth mother's baby could not be ours. He would not permit it, because he could not allow us to solicit this birth mother–while "captive" in our house–to favor us with her choice.

The girl in question was just 18, living with her parents. The parents knew the situation, but they were unwilling for their conservative extended family, their neighbors, friends, or the school kids to know. The baby was due in three months; she needed housing *now*. Earlier, we had heard that the waiting time for an appointment with attorney Schrybman was at least two months. Now he was telling us, David and me, "I've got to know a lot more about you. Can you come to my office on Friday?"

We could. We did. We had a four-hour meeting with him, to learn all about private adoption through an attorney, and how he practiced; what is legal, what is not, and what he would expect from us–both as temporary hosts to a pregnant teenager and as private-adoption clients in his practice.

The following week, we met both the girl and the girl's father. On Saturday, the father brought his daughter to live with us for the interim. She was very pleasant. Her boyfriend was still very much in the picture. When her time came to deliver, it would be the boyfriend who would rush to our house and drive her to the hospital. They were very young, but apparently had yielded to their parents' "good sense"–to allow the baby to be adopted into a good home–so they could finish growing up.

We enjoyed having "Mary" in our home. We learned a lot from her about what a birth mother might think and feel, what kinds of questions she would want to have answered before she would give her baby forever to another. We were privileged to overhear some of her questions to prospective adoptive parents, as she interviewed them over the telephone.

Early one morning, Mary called her boyfriend. "It's time," she said. "Come fast!"

He came quickly, but almost not quickly enough. We learned later that he had stopped off to grab a cup of coffee on his way to our house. Then he picked up Mary and rushed her to the hospital. After the baby was born, he went back out to his truck and found the coffee, still in its holder–and still warm.

Meanwhile, our attorney was placing ads in several suburban newspapers on our behalf.

Adoption–We are a loving couple
who can't have children of our own.
We can help with your expenses.
Please call us collect 301-587-xxxx

or write us, David & Pam Blair,
P.O. Box xxxx, Silver Spring, MD
20901. Let's help each other.

Following his instructions, we had obtained a second telephone line in our home, this one was strictly unlisted and in the name of a fictitious "nephew" who—we told the telephone company—would be staying with us for an extended time and who needed a private telephone line of his own.

We also got a post office box, obtained for us at third hand by another person—a friend of a friend—who was unknown to us. That friend twice-removed went to the post office and hired a post office box in her own name, adding to her box's "ownership" record our own fictitious names—David Blair and Pam Blair. These were the names with which we interacted with expectant birth mothers.

As our attorney explained it, Maryland law requires that the names of adoptive parents are not be disclosed to birth parents, and he expected us *strictly* to follow the law. This, of course, also served our own interest of ensuring that no angry relative of the birth mother—or even the birth mother herself—could ever trouble us with misgivings, once the adoption was final.

When a birth mother would call, answering our ad, David Blair and Pam Blair were the names we gave. When we were asked (and we *were* asked) if these were our real names, we replied that the first names were our real names, but the surname was fictitious—as our attorney had instructed us, in compliance with state law.

Once we had talked to a birth mother, our job—said our attorney—was to get the birth mother to call a second time and, ultimately, to arrange a meeting at, say, a fast food restaurant. We would then go to the restaurant to meet the birth mother.

Did they all show up? No, they did not all show up. The very first time, we made a date to meet a birth mother in Annapolis, the state capital, about 40 miles away. We waited, we waited, and we waited. She never showed. (Nor did she ever call.) I was devastated. I couldn't believe that this could happen. I was so crushed that I started to go on pessimistically about never finding a baby to love, etc.

David was more practical. He said that these things could happen. People could change their minds, they did often enough, even when the psychological stakes were much smaller than when a baby is involved. He wanted to end the wait by having dinner and going home. I agreed, but only if he would first drive us to another restaurant. I said that I did not want her to show up in the middle of our meal. At this point, years later, I wonder if it also was because I did not want the feeling of having been rejected as a potential mother. Maybe I wanted to feel that the final closing of that particular door was my own.

After this experience, we decided that we would always plan, after we had met with a prospective birth mother, to have our own private dinner out, before returning home. That way, we figured, even if the birth mother failed to show up, at least part of our excursion would still come to pass; our trip would not be in vain, because our final plan for the evening would always be fulfilled. That was important to me. With a reward at the end of the evening, regardless, I would not be devastated by a "no show."

We put to rest the idea that there were no babies to be had by older adoptive couples. Over a three-month period, we were offered, actually *offered*–not counting people who didn't show up or who changed their minds–*seven* babies.

Our attorney began to be angry with us: "You two are being too picky," he said. I think, because he had been an adoptive child himself, he had very strong feelings about adoption. He just wanted to get these babies good homes. He had little patience for a couple who wanted a baby "*so* bad," but didn't accept the first baby offered.

Well, why were we so "picky?" More than one reason.

One birth mother was an immigrant from Mexico, who was working as a housekeeper for a college professor–who apparently had seduced her into a relationship which resulted in her pregnancy. She had children back in Mexico to whom she regularly sent money. The shame of bearing a child in another country, to a man not her husband, was a great humiliation to her–more than she could accept. We met her at her friend's house, who translated for us. We went home and talked it over. While we wanted that child, soon to be born, I was worried that there might be members of our extended families who would not fully accept a child of different ethnicity than their own.

The lady's friend called us, wanting to know our intentions. She berated us, saying that we had disappointed and shamed her friend. The friend said that the mother-to-be, being a woman of tiny stature, was sure that her baby had been rejected for an expectation of its being too small, too short.

Suitably scolded and sad, we pushed on.

Another young woman lived 35 miles away, in Baltimore. We went to see her, and we shared a lunch. She was a very attractive woman, with the most beautiful eyes I have ever seen. To our questions about the father, she informed us she had been raped, gang-raped in fact. The father was one of about seven men. I am not sure after all these years, but she may have said that there were either drugs or alcohol involved in her rape. We were concerned. If she were an alcoholic or drug addict, that did not augur well for a fully healthy baby. Not only that, but I came to realize that, when our baby grew up enough to ask about his/her birth father, the only thing we knew, the only thing we could tell our child about the father, was that he was a rapist. We also did not follow up this opportunity. We probably said something like, "We'll talk it over and get back to you."

When we did not get back to her, she called us, late on Saturday night, sounding desperate. She demanded to know our decision. When we failed to give her a clear and confident answer, she became angry, and we finally had to close the conversation a bit sternly and awkwardly. Another sad experience for all. Another lovely woman whom we felt we could not help.

There was another young girl. After receiving her call, we drove a great distance into the country to meet her at an Arby's restaurant. Afterwards, we drove by her boyfriend's home and talked with him briefly, as he stood near our car. We rather liked both the girl and her boyfriend. There didn't seem to be anything wrong with either of them, beyond probably some youthful indiscretion. The next day, we tried to call her, without success. We tried again, and again. Finally, we reached her at her parents' home on Thanksgiving Day. There seemed to be a house full of relatives. She answered the call to the phone, but it was evident she was very uncomfortable talking to us. She said they had decided to keep the baby.

I could not even *start* to talk a birth mother out of a baby that she has decided to keep; my conscience tells me that one shouldn't even try. So, we withdrew from that. We thought that perhaps her family had somehow become involved and nixed her plans of adoption. Well, good for them. Perhaps the baby would be born into a loving extended family, and the young parents would find support. We hoped so.

One day, it was a man who called. I was alone at home to take the call—David was still on his way home from work. This man said, to be brief about it, that his wife was pregnant and that I could have their baby if I would agree to have sex with the man until the baby was born. Well! We had been instructed firmly by attorney Schrybman that we were *not* to reject any baby over the phone, that we had *one and only one* responsibility whenever anyone answered our ad: *get the party to call back again*!

So, I told the man that I could not give him an answer; I would have to talk to my husband about it. My husband would be home within an hour; he should call us back after seven o'clock. Obviously, whatever David was going to say, this man's idea of a suitable arrangement was never going to be suitable to me. But I wanted David to deal with this.

When David got home, I told him this story. He immediately said that the man, in all likelihood, was a complete fraud. "If we were to give him what he wants, it is likely that we would never really see a baby." When the man called back, David answered the phone—and that was that.

Then one day, another man called. His wife was pregnant, he said, and they could not afford another child. We talked briefly and we agreed to meet for lunch at a certain roadside restaurant about 40 miles from our home.

"How will we recognize you?" David asked.

"Well, I'm six feet six, and I'll be wearing a cowboy hat."

So we met Jim and Belva. They already had a boy and a girl. Belva was a homemaker and Jim a truck driver. Their means were modest, but their family was intact. We decided they were the salt of the earth, and we wanted their baby—due in just six weeks.

Just as instructed, we contacted our attorney immediately. Mr. Schrybman promptly got in touch with the birth parents, and met with them multiple times to ensure that they understood the requirements of the state adoption law and how everything would be handled—just as he had taught us. There would be a contract between the birth and adoptive parents, but the birth parents would have the right for a definite period of time to change their mind and back out. After the birth, and after examination by doctors and observation by nurses for a couple of days, to be sure the baby was normal and healthy, we the adoptive parents would come to the hospital and meet our attorney, who would see that the transfer of the baby to our possession and care was done smoothly, sensitively, and according to law. Once we had received the baby, the birth parents had the right for 90 days to require its return.

The law prevented us from making any payment for the baby, but we could and would pay for all the expenses, including prenatal care and every expense of the birth.

As it happened, the couple had medical insurance from the birth father's employment, so our expenses for baby and mother were minimal. Also, they lived within moderate driving distance—and in the same state—so our travel and accommodations costs were low. All of this was fortunate. If the baby had been born out of state, there might have been complications from different state laws—requiring the involvement of an additional attorney. There could be airline fares, extended hotel stays, etc.

Once everybody was "on the same page," with whatever legal arrangements were necessary, our attorney had counseled us that it would be really smart to invite the birth parents to share another meal with us, to "celebrate" our arrangement. "Take them to a nice restaurant," he said, "and have a good time." He even gave us a recommendation for the restaurant. He had arranged other adoptions in that town, so he knew his way around a bit.

Before parting, I asked our attorney, "When can I get excited?" He replied, "When the baby is in your arms—*and not a minute before!*"

We had a very enjoyable dinner with the birth parents, at the Red Horse Steakhouse, in Frederick, Maryland. We learned a bit more about our new "friends." They had been high school sweethearts. Jim had played football. After graduation, he was in the Navy and had enjoyed his travels to various scenes. We particularly remembered his expressed interest in having visited Athens, Greece, and the museums there. We thought, "That's great. Jim seems a guy with above average intelligence and interest in the world, for the amount of education he's had." That gave us even more confidence that we had chosen well—that our baby would have a good heritage.

At the end of the dinner, Belva said, "I have something to give you—for the baby." When we left the restaurant, we walked with them to their car. From the trunk of the car, Jim retrieved an *enormous* cloth laundry bag, packed full of baby clothes. Belva said, "If there are any clothes here that you can't use, like boy clothes for a girl or girl clothes for a boy, you can give them back to me for my sisters." We promised we would, thanked her profusely, and carried the bag of clothes to our car.

Then we happened to see; just before they drove away, that Belva took something out of her purse and lit up a cigarette! We were shocked and dismayed. "She smokes!" We wondered how much she smoked. She had apparently suppressed her urge to smoke in the restaurant, not even lighting up at the end of the meal, as smokers often do. We wondered if she knew about reports that smoking could be harmful to unborn babies, and whether she had suppressed her urge to smoke as long as she could, in deference to our supposed feelings or fears.

The delivery of the baby was expected for February 28, 1986, but it didn't come that soon. Finally, the doctors scheduled induced labor for March 12, and we were instructed to come to the hospital that day at 8 AM.

I had asked Belva where she would like me to be when she went into the hospital for the birth. She invited me to be in the delivery room—a great honor and privilege for me; I can always know that there has never been a moment of our child's life that I have not shared.

Meanwhile, David was waiting (where else?) in the waiting room. The labor was fairly short, but to us quite long—a little over three hours. A woman in the waiting room struck up a conversation with David, asking what brought him to the hospital that day. Our attorney had instructed us that, in many cases, some of the birth mother's relatives turn out to strongly oppose her plan for adoption, and such relatives are often present in the hospital for the birth. Also, in small town hospitals especially, even the staff may have strong feelings against adoption, or at least against private adoption—arranged by attorneys—thinking that there is something shady about adoption by that means. In any case—to avoid any unpleasant confrontation—we had been advised that we should not identify ourselves in the hospital as adoptive parents. In our case, we knew that some members of Belva's family *were* unsupportive.

So, David replied to the woman in the waiting room that he was just there to accompany a friend. Minutes later, I appeared and announced boldly to David, *"Congratulations, you have a son!"*

That afternoon, after our baby boy was snugly secured in the nursery, we got to see him through the glass. He was precious, snoozing peacefully, wrapped up snugly with a little knit cap on his head. Belva's own mother was there as well, and we met her as she also admired the little guy through the glass.

That was about all there was for us to do at the hospital that day, so we went out to have a lunch and then to a movie, *The Color Purple*, before retiring to our hotel for the night.

As it happened, Belva's mother was on the hospital's cleaning staff, and when we arrived the second morning, we saw her briskly polishing the front entry lobby as we walked through. At some point, the birth father arrived—just returned from his overnight interstate truck run—bringing his son, about eight, and two-year old daughter with him. He had not seen the baby and was planning not to see him. He and his children had visited Belva in the maternity ward, and for a time we sat with them in a lounge area, watching the daytime *Wheel Of Fortune* program on the TV. Jim was a very quick solver of the word puzzles, and again I was impressed with his evident intelligence. Jim's son Eugene was visibly upset when he met us; he clearly did not want to lose his baby brother. I spoke with young Eugene, wanting to comfort him. I assured him that we were going to love his little brother as much as he did himself, and we would give little Andrew the best care that anyone ever could. I think he was soothed, a little; his tears abated somewhat.

The little girl, Crystal, was too young, probably, to comprehend the situation.

Since we were only 40 miles from home, it seemed just as convenient to return home the second night and return to the hospital the next morning.

On the third day, Friday, we met our attorney at the hospital, who informed us that, once again, Belva's mother was present in the hospital. He took me to the nursery area to collect the baby Andrew and his things, instructing David to bring the car to the entrance and wait for me and the baby. After supervising the transfer of Andrew to my arms and possession, Mr. Schrybman went off, as he said, to distract the grandmother and avoid any last minute encounter. I emerged from the hospital's front door, David secured baby Andrew into his new car seat, and off we went−bound for a wonderful life's adventure.

As soon as we arrived at our home, we set about making our precious Andrew comfortable in his bassinette and stocking the refrigerator with eight bottles of baby formula, each ready to be fitted with a nipple and fed, without a moment's delay, as needed. Imagine our thrill at our new parenthood. Home at last!

The joy and worry and expense of raising a child to adulthood had begun. Everything had gone smoothly to this point, and the financial cost of our adoption had been quite modest, relatively speaking. Our expenses amounted to several thousand dollars for our attorney's *many* professional services, one night at a hotel, a few dinners out, and a few hundred miles on our car. The reward was: our perfect baby, *Andrew Silverwood Hack*, and the promised fulfillment of our mutual, lifelong dream!

GROWING UP YEARS

My Mom and Dad were wonderful parents; their love and caretaking of me has made all the difference in my life, right up to this present day. When our Andrew came to live with us, pending official adoption, I was extremely glad that I had finally come to the point where I could "pay it forward" to Andrew–that is, I could now begin to repay my parents by doing my best to ensure that Andrew would always have opportunities comparable to mine, and a life just as happy and fulfilled.

On Andrew's second day with us, a Saturday, one of the pediatric nurses from Walter Reed came to our home, volunteering her own time to teach us how to "bathe the baby."

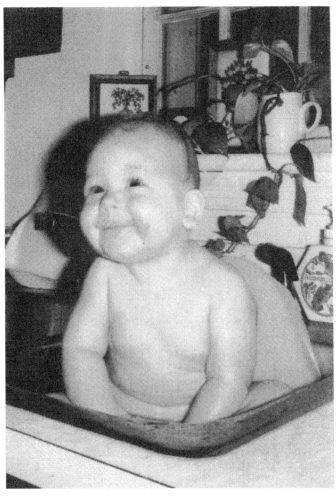

Andrew enjoying his bath at a few months of age, looking adoringly at, who else? His nanny!

PE Tubes

Andrew developed a number of medical concerns. Among the first were the ear infections. I don't know how many trips we took to the pediatrician to have his ears examined, yet again, and to renew his antibiotic prescriptions.

Finally, we took him to the National Children's Medical Center (Children's Hospital) in Washington, D.C., near our Silver Spring, Maryland, home. Over the years, Andrew received something like five different sets of PE tubes or pressure-equalizing tubes—tiny plastic devices resting upon and penetrating his eardrums to allow drainage and prevent permanent hearing loss. Five sets, because from time to time one or more of the ear tubes would fall out or become plugged. Counting trips to surgery for removal of tubes, Andrew underwent general anesthesia something like seven times.

There's nothing very serious that can go wrong with the actual surgery involved in implanting, removing or replacing an ear tube; it's a very simple procedure that may not even draw blood. But remember that I worked for 28 years in a hospital. So every time Andrew had to experience general anesthesia, I was a wreck until I saw him in the recovery room, coming out of it.

The very first time we visited Andrew in the recovery room, another child nearby had a toy with a ratchet mechanism that made an intense buzzing sound.

"TOO LOUD!!" Andrew shouted! Wow! Did those ear tubes really work! As soon as he was conscious, he could hear EVER so much better!

Once, David was coming down the stairs, only to encounter Andrew coming up the stairs to meet him. Raising both arms above his shoulders beseechingly, Andrew demanded, "Up-ba! Up-ba!" As a speech pathologist, of course, I was keenly concerned that my baby son learn the proper pronunciation of all the sounds of speech. So, I had begun modeling speech for him with those sounds that are easiest for the very young to make. The "plosives," b and p especially, are very easy to imitate, involving, as they do, the lips pursed together, followed by an "explosion" of expelled air. The essential placement of these speech sounds is on the lips, where a young child can easily see them to imitate. Thus, in mimicking my _exaggerated_ plosive sound, Andrew had learned to say "up" as up-_ba!_

Now, standing on the stairs, looking _way_ up to Daddy's face, arms up in anticipation of a big lift by Daddy, Andrew was demanding, "Up-ba! Up-ba." There was something about the insistence of Andrew's demand that moved David to reply "Up, _Please!_" Andrew didn't miss a beat: "Up-ba _pease!_ Up-ba _pease!_

Clearly, we had not yet worked much on the "_L_," one of the very hardest sounds to imitate.

Bedtime

One time, with guests in our living room– engaged in after-dinner conversation–David took toddler Andrew upstairs to put him to bed. Once changed into his bedclothes, Andrew settled into

David's arms for a bedtime story. David decided to tell the story of the *Three Little Pigs*. You know, the one about the three houses—one of straw, one of sticks, and one of bricks?

Well, the story went pretty well. When David got to the point where the wolf says, "I'll huff, and I'll puff, 'til I blow your house down," David started going: "HUFF, PUFF, Huff, Puff, huff, puff, huff, puff; huff, puff ...., ..., ..., ..., ..." and so on, and so on, and so on—until Andrew fell, finally, f-a-s-t a-s-l-e-e-p.

Well! That worked so well that David thought he had found a sure-fire way to get Andrew to bed and asleep, with no extra fuss. But the technique worked only about one more time, after that. Soon enough, when David would ask if Andrew wanted to hear the story of the three little pigs again, Andrew would say, "No." It seemed that he somehow got it—realized that if he wanted all the time with Daddy that he could get, it would have to be some other story!

David's favorite picture of young Andrew.

Once Andrew was well-started in nursery school, our bedtime routine typically consisted of asking Andrew to tell us one good thing and one not-so-good thing that happened that day "at school." We had come to realize that it was pointless to query Andrew, for instance, with "What did you do at school today." That was just too big a question; it was overwhelming. Like most kids, he was likely to say, "Nothing." Instead, we started asking him to tell us just "one good thing" about the day, and then "one not-so-good thing" about the day. Sometimes he would have specific answers to both questions, but just as often he might say, "Nothing not-so-good happened today." When we got that answer, we thought that perhaps we were doing something right.

Our asking Andrew for the good and not-so-good things happening in his life was very intentional. We wanted Andrew to know that he could talk to us about *anything* happening in his life, the good and the bad. I think we had pretty good communication as he was growing up, and I credit that to our early start at talking about *"anything."* Now that he is 30-plus, he (amazingly) still calls us for advice. He apparently still thinks we are capable of *good* advice. David says he wishes that he had been able to have such confidence in parental advice, at any age.

When Andrew was a little older, we tried to make it a practice to "catch him being good." Parents often think that their job is to notice and correct "bad" behavior in children, but they often take good behavior for granted, letting it pass without mention. We resolved to make it an explicit practice to notice and to praise behaviors that we wanted to encourage, to reinforce. As an example: "Did I just see you sharing your toy with your friend? That is very good, Andrew. You make me very proud of you when you do that!"

Marfan Syndrome Tests

When Andrew was about four years old, David took him to see his pediatrician, Dr. Hubbard, for his regular checkup. After the exam, Dr. Hubbard asked to talk to David alone. For the first time, she told him/us that she had been paying careful attention for a period of time to Andrew's heart sounds. There was some evidence of some sort of heart murmur or irregularity, she said. She had not mentioned it until she had monitored it over more than one regular exam, but now she felt it was time to refer Andrew to Children's Hospital, in Washington D.C., for some advanced and specific tests. Because of Andrew's top-of-the-chart height for his age, the length of his long bones, and his heart sounds, she wanted to have him worked-up to "rule out" a possible diagnosis of Marfan Syndrome.

Marfan Syndrome is characterized by a number of physical characteristics, including a tendency to grow very tall, to have long thin fingers, and to develop heart problems and vision problems[41]

When we went to Children's Hospital, we were seen first at the Cardiology Department and then the

---

[41] Abraham Lincoln was sometimes suspected, long after his death in 1865, to have been born with Marfan Syndrome. The adult Lincoln was six feet four inches in height and exhibited a few other characteristics associated with Marfan Syndrome. More recently, Lincoln has been suspected instead to have had something else—perhaps a genetic inheritance known as Multiple Endocrine Neoplasia, Type 2B (MEN2B). *—www.physical-lincoln.com/diagnosis.html (Retrieved August 21, 2016). This controversy* could be resolved through DNA analysis of "blood relics" of Lincoln. At this writing in 2016—so far as we can determine—such analysis has never been accomplished.

Genetics Department. The result of these visits proved inconclusive. Then we were sent for a test that we were told would tell us the final answer, Pediatric Ophthalmology. When the ophthalmologist was through testing Andrew, the answer was that, no, Andrew did not have the Marfan Syndrome after all—though he exhibited several of the characteristics.

Andrew's social development began to take off when we enrolled him, at about the age of two, at Kensington Day Care—a pre-school extending through Kindergarten. The clientele of Kensington was rather diverse, and he began to fit in well. When he had a sleep-over, it tended to seem like a caucus of the United Nations.

The diversity of Andrew's social experience continued with enrollment for first grade at New Hampshire Estates Elementary School, and later its counterpart for third through sixth grades, Oakview Elementary School.

When Andrew was 13, we took him on his first Ocean Cruise, from Spain through Gibraltar and Morocco, ending at Lisbon Portugal. Then we took an overnight train from Lisbon to Madrid, and traveled by rented car from Madrid to the Costa del Sol and back again. From Madrid we flew to Paris, where Andrew climbed to the top of the Eiffel Tower, with some high school age boys we met in the waiting line. It may be no surprise to the reader that David and I took the elevator the whole way, and we met Andrew at the top!

After a round-trip to Lyon by bullet train, where we saw a representative country chateau, we flew from Paris home again.

Thornton Friends School

For middle school, we wanted to get Andrew into what we hoped would be a more academically challenging school than our local public middle school, so, on a tip from a friend, we interviewed and placed Andrew at Thornton Friends Middle School.

Evidently, our vetting of the school wasn't thorough enough, because it turned out to be not quite what we assumed. Over Andrew's seventh and eighth grade years, we gradually came to realize that Thornton Friends was not exactly a school for high achieving youngsters. Rather, many of the kids at Thornton were there because their parents wanted a school where their child could get a lot of personal attention, in an attempt to deal with adjustment problems the child had exhibited elsewhere. In this environment, Andrew became a virtual star, socially speaking, His relationship skills exceeded those exhibited by many of the others—but we never found there the environment of high-achieving peer relationships and role models that we had sought.

Nevertheless, Andrew had some unique opportunities at Thornton. He eventually joined the school chorus, with which he sang at the lighting of the National Christmas Tree and met First Lady Hillary Clinton. Later, he traveled on a performance tour to Paris and Belgium. In Paris, revisiting the Eiffel Tower, he was proud to display his worldliness by leading his fellow choristers on an ascent—his second—of that celebrated landmark. In Belgium, he fainted in the course of a performance at the NATO Headquarters complex. Needless to say, David and I were rather concerned when we received a call about that, but it amounted to nothing much—apparently just a consequence of heat, fatigue and dehydration.

In his Middle School years Andrew also traveled, twice over the summers, with a church group led by Thornton Friends teachers and parents—to the Pine Ridge Indian Reservation in South Dakota—where he and his friends repaired and painted buildings and led Daily Vacation Bible School classes on the Reservation.

After Andrew's 7th and 8th grade years at Thornton Friends School, he enrolled for high school at our local public high school, Montgomery Blair. After Andrew's first year of high school, we three traveled through Alaska and Canada's Yukon Territory by tour bus and narrow-gauge railroad. In his junior and senior years, he was bused for half of the day to Thomas Edison High School of Technology, where he studied Digital Electronics and Computer Networking.

In the summer of 2003, Andrew flew alone to California to visit for three weeks with David's family. While Andrew was away, David and I flew to Buenos Aires and then to Iguazu Falls, which we saw from both sides of the river Parana', which divides Argentina from Brazil. Overlooking the Falls, David enthused, "If this is a ten, Niagara is a four!"

In 2005, we all made the trip to Athens and the Greek Islands that I described earlier—Crete, Mikonos, Santorini, Rhodes, followed by the ancient or modern cities of Ephesus, Rome, Florence, and Venice.

In 2008, with Andrew out of high school and working in Myrtle Beach, South Carolina, David and I flew to China, where we saw the customary things, including the Great Wall and the Terra Cotta Soldiers.

A Rough Year And More

The year 2011 was a year of surgeries and sadness. First, David had a hip replacement surgery in February, followed by a painful series of dislocations of his new hip. In April, my Mom died. (The year before, she had been diagnosed with uterine cancer, of which she said immediately, "I don't want anything done. I've had a wonderful life, but it is enough!") In June, Andrew had surgery to replace the aortic valve in his heart, dealing finally with that unusual heart sound that his pediatrician had identified years earlier. The following year, I had a knee replacement surgery which took a long, long time for its ultimate benefits to be realized in terms of reduced pain.

Andrew Meets His Birth Mother

Once Andrew graduated from high school, I asked him if he would like to meet his birth mother. "Yes," he said, "Of course. Definitely!"

So, we made a date to meet Belva at the very same restaurant in Frederick, Maryland, where David and I met Belva and Jim for the first time: The Barbara Fritchie Restaurant. By this time, though, Belva and Jim had divorced, Belva was re-married, and Andrew had a younger half-bother, Robert, by this second marriage. This new nuclear family came, all together, to meet Andrew.

The first thing Belva said to Andrew was, "I want you to know, I've always loved you." There couldn't have been a more perfect thing to say, I thought, since so many adopted children seem to worry or at least wonder why they were "given up," and what that may say about their birth parent or the birth parent's feelings toward the child.

As we were all about to depart the restaurant, Belva turned to me and said, "I'd do it again, but only with you!' I hear that still, in my head, from time to time; I think it was the finest compliment I've ever heard.

That meeting went about as well as we could have imagined or hoped, and I was especially glad it occurred, because a few years later, with Andrew in his mid-twenties, Belva died. We learned of her death just two days before her funeral was scheduled to occur. I called Andrew, and as soon as he heard about the funeral, he said, "I'm going!"

We said, "We'll meet you there!"

David and I met Andrew, early the day of the funeral. Andrew had driven up to West Virginia from his home in South Carolina, while David and I drove from our home in Maryland. When we entered the church, a couple of heads turned, and we imagined someone thinking, *Could that tall young man be baby Andrew?* Andrew, by that time, was six-feet-five. (Remember that his birth father was six-six.)

After the service, we learned that, indeed, someone was thinking exactly what I imagined, for a young mother came up to us, asked us a question, then turned to her two little girls and said, "Girls, this is your uncle Andy!"

We were all accepted just as warmly—into the presence of this bereaved extended family—as was Andrew. Andrew met also his young half-brother

Robert, his older brother "Eugene"–who was now in the U.S. Army and had adopted for himself the new name, Clarence–and his sister Crystal, herself now a mother of two. We learned what we could of Belva's last illness, and we later speculated that economic circumstances and health care of unknown kind after her divorce may have figured in her death, at the

Andrew at six feet FIVE.

relatively early age of 57. It underlined for all of us the benefit of Andrew's being adopted into a *second* loving family—one well-enough off to provide a high level of health care for his several medical problems, besides myriad development opportunities for his latent talents. Not less important is a *birth family* who also loved him, remembered him, and treasured the memory enough to accept his and our presence among them without reservation—even after twenty-something years apart.

By that time, Andrew had been working for several years as a member of The Geek Squad at the Best Buy store in Myrtle Beach, South Carolina. A couple of years later, he changed jobs to Apple Inc. and became a Home Technical Advisor—coaching the owners of new Apple computers and iPhones on how to use their devices, working from his own home office.

By 2015, Andrew's further career development brought him to begin working in the Apple Store in Charleston, South Carolina, where he continues at this writing.

Andrew once said that David "taught me everything I know" about computers. David says, "That is the sweetest lie I ever heard,"[42] because, he says, "There was a time when I taught Andrew everything *I* knew *at that time* about computers—but he has gone far beyond me—*he is my guru now*!" Andrew also says, from time to time, that we "did everything right" in raising him. That is of course not quite true. Certainly we *tried* to do everything right, and we know that we didn't always succeed. But to have him think that—or at least *say* that—is what every parent would love to hear, and so seldom ever does. From that time forward until today, I have heard him saying that phrase, in my head, EVERY DAY.

[42] The phrase comes from the 1996 film, *Mr. Holland's Opus:*

Mr. Holland: "Look, you... you tell me that... we're gonna have a baby. Well...that's like... falling in love with John Coltrane ... all over again."

Mrs. Holland: "If that is a lie, that is the sweetest lie I ever heard."

—http://www.subzin.com/quotes/M12879a882/Mr.+Holland% 27s+Opus/that%27s+like...+falling+in+love+with+John+Coltr ane...

Retrieved June 5, 2015.

LEADERSHIP AND MANAGEMENT
DEVELOPMENT

Somehow, I learned that there was going to be available a week-long training class at Walter Reed on "Leadership and Management Development" (LMDC). I thought, *Well–that sounds neat!* So I asked my boss, and he said, "Sure, go ahead."

Things had been kind of routine lately; I needed something new to keep things interesting. But I never gave a thought to ever being in charge of anything. That never crossed my mind. I wasn't a Ph.D or an M.D., and most of the bigwigs at Walter Reed were "doctors." Anyway, I didn't want it! To be Supervisor of Speech Pathology would be so time-consuming, so stressful, that it didn't appeal in the least. My thing was treating patients. But the prospect of taking that course just seemed like a "little ray of sunshine!"

So I took the class. Loved it! Learned a lot from it. Then one of the co-facilitators came to me, saying, "We need to train some new facilitators; would you be interested in taking the training, a month's training, to become a co-facilitator?"

"Sure. If my boss... I don't think my boss would let me. You'll have to ask him, if you want me to do it.... Yes, you will have to ask my boss if I can do it. It can't come from me." The trainer said that he'd be glad to do that, and what do you know? My boss agreed! (He always agreed!)

The first class, the subject matter class, had been a week. The training to become a facilitator was a month! I thought learning to become a facilitator of the Leadership and Management Development training class would be wonderful! I had already taken the Death and Dying seminar, and I loved that; I just happened to love group dynamics. So I thought, *Yeah!* and Bill gave me permission to do it, so I did it.

In the first class, it had been a stressful week, because you were always "on." It was a small group, and everything was very experiential. Everything you did was analyzed. "Why didn't she raise her hand?" "So-and-so is taking over!" We were analyzing our own group's process, not just *talking* about leadership *and leadership avoidance* in the abstract. "Why do you think the group did that" "How could that have worked better?" Looking at group dynamics, big time. Absolutely! It was somewhat similar to a group therapy process. We had people in tears, because they were learning about themselves, very fast, in ways that were difficult for them. There would be two people getting into conflict, because they were both trying to take over leadership of the group. "Why do you suppose he's upset," or "Why do you suppose she's taking over." It was just a real group-dynamics situation.

The *month-long* class was even *more* tense, but it was very well planned out, with every exercise well mapped. We trainees collected files of handouts to use in our later teaching. There were different modules. We learned to teach the importance of feedback–to solicit feedback from one's subordinates and to regard feedback, *even negative feedback*, as a *gift*. We learned the ten behaviors or "rules" of a good supervisor.

Ten Rules for Good Supervision

1. Set good examples.

2. Say what you mean and mean what you say.

3. Maintain open, two-way communication channels.

4. Take responsibility for your own feelings and behaviors.

5. Be sensitive to the particular needs of individuals within the work group.

6. Trust in the strength and wisdom of the work group.

7. Create your action plan around *goals*, not around the available methods or resources.

8. Keep performance counseling separate from personal counseling.

9. Adapt your management style to the maturity level of the individual employee.

10. Treat your employee as you would like your boss to treat you.

It was a great and powerful experience and one of the best investments of time and effort I ever made. But that month was *so* stressful. My mother came to visit with us in our new home, while I was taking the class; altogether, I was so stressed out that, for the first time in my life, I came down with hives!

But thank God I took those classes, because they helped me. Even though I never dreamed that I would become head of the section, thank God that–when I did–I had taken those courses beforehand.

WHEN I BECAME CHIEF

It all began when Bill (my supervisor) was on vacation. Since I was senior to everyone except Bill, I was the Acting Supervisor of the section. One of the doctors asked me what was happening with a case in which they had requested our consultation, they had not received a report. As Bill's most senior subordinate, I was responsible for assigning consults to clinicians. So, I went to my list of assignments and found that I had assigned that patient to Bill.

When I went to find out what Bill had done about it, I found, all over his desk, about *two dozen* consult requests on which Bill had never acted. Here were a huge number of patients that had never even been *seen* by Speech Pathology, despite their attending physicians having requested our evaluation of their cases. About two dozen consults were just sitting on his desk, and he was apparently doing nothing about them. That was just inexcusable. I felt obligated to the soldiers of Viet Nam. I had to call Bill's boss, the Director of the Army Audiology and Speech Center, Colonel Rodney Atack. I told him what I had found. "What should I do," I said. He replied, "I'll take it from here. As Bill's subordinate, I appreciated Colonel Atack's taking me out of the loop of having discovered my own supervisor in a situation of malfeasance.

Well, Colonel Atack not only went to see what was on Bill's desk, but he took his Assistant Director with him, as a witness, because he knew it was going to be a matter of importance. It was not much later that Bill was demoted: when Bill came back from vacation, Colonel Atack relieved him of his supervisory duties.

Colonel Atack said that he would ask Bill to vacate his office so that I could move into it. I told the colonel that I didn't want Bill to have to vacate his office; I said that I could do the job from the office that I was in. Soon after, I called Bill into my office and said, "Look, I didn't ask for this to happen, and you didn't ask for this to happen. But let's just agree to make the best of the situation, and try to make it a positive experience for both of us." Bill said, "Absolutely"–and that was that.

But then, Bill got a lawyer to contest or appeal his demotion, and there was eventually a hearing before an administrative law judge. The hearing scared me to death. I was SO uncomfortable. I never knew that all this was going to happen when I told Colonel Atack to look at Bill's desk. There was a lawyer for Walter Reed, I guess. There was Colonel Atack and me, and Bill, and Bill's lawyer.

At one point, Bill offered a claim that someone had used his computer to delete his records of having seen all of the patients that he was accused of not having seen. When his lawyer asked me if I knew anything about that, I countered by asking Bill whether he had ever given his computer password to anyone else. When he said he had not, I asked him how he thought anyone could have tampered with his computer records. Bill had no answer to that.

During a fire drill, with many of the participants gathered together outdoors, the judge said to all present (excepting Bill, who was not present) that "Miss Silverwood is asking the best questions."

When the result of the hearing was filed, Bill's demotion was confirmed.

It wasn't a comfortable situation. Here was the man who had been my boss for 22 years, who had hired me as a twenty-something, had approved practically everything I ever did or requested or proposed over that period. Now I was *his* boss, near the end of his career. It had to feel very awkward for him. It was surely awkward for me. But Bill didn't stay long after that. Soon after the final decision was rendered, Bill announced his decision to retire.

Bill Simpkins was a very nice person. He was also very suggestible. When I had interviewed with him for my job, years earlier, Blanche Schnapper–his subordinate–said, "Hire her!" and he did, practically on the spot. He was a procrastinator. He got out of doing his job by delegating everything. He spent a lot of time just socializing, both on and off the phone. One example is his having appointed *me* to make assignments of patients to our various clinicians.

Once Bill was demoted, Colonel Atack chose ME to replace Bill, as permanent section supervisor! I was flummoxed! I had never expected that. Colonel Atack was a Ph.D. in audiology, and I expected that he would want to recruit a Ph.D in speech pathology to head the Speech Section, in keeping with his often-stated objective to raise standards generally in the Center.

I had truly never expected this to happen. I was flattered beyond belief that Colonel Atack thought I could do it. But I said to myself, Wait a minute Pam. You've been here 22 years! You're training leaders at Walter Reed in how to be better leaders! You know what it takes to be a good supervisor. You're teaching how to be a good supervisor!

But I had to ask David what he thought about all this. I needed to be sure I wasn't taking on something that might diminish my roles as wife and mother.

I said I'd like to think about it overnight. Then I went home to talk to David. I still remember what I said.

"Do you think I should take this job?"

David was very supportive. About all he said was, "You can do this, Pam." He may also have said, "You go girl!"

Colonel Rodney Atack

Colonel Atack was the best supervisor I ever had. Of course, at first he had been Bill's supervisor, when Bill was my supervisor. But after the change, I reported directly to Colonel Atack.

I always felt supported and respected by him. He had a good sense of humor and he cared deeply for the agency and for the people within it. He was a real people person, and he cared deeply for how things were impacting on me, as well as how things were impacting on the section. He truly was all-encompassing. He was concerned for the people below him as well as the people above him. He was wonderful. He always worked hard to make things better. He was a very sensitive and thoughtful, caring human being. He was a one-of-a- kind person—an exceptional human being. He had wonderful people skills. He set very good examples. He was always on-time and at-work. He followed the rule that I learned in LMDC: *Say what you mean and mean what you say*. He would often ask what was going on in my life, before talking business. If he was wrong, he would admit it. He was sensitive to individuals. An example is how he just took charge of that situation involving Bill's desktop. He took responsibility for handling that, getting me completely out of what was going to be a touchy situation. When it was time for performance counseling, it was *just* performance counseling–unconfused by any personal comments. He treated me like an equal, but he always showed that he cared.

Although Colonel Atack never said so, I do believe that my having had that LMDC course, and then in addition taking the training to *teach* it, played a part in my being selected as Supervisor after Bill was demoted. Also, I had helped Colonel Atack defend his decision to demote Bill. By testifying in the hearing, I had helped him "get the goods" on Bill (by asking the right questions in the hearing) but I never wanted to be the Supervisor; that was the furthest thing from my mind.

I continued as Supervisor of Speech Pathology for six more years. In the meantime, there was another national election, a change in political administration, and another of those periodic pushes (yet again) to downsize the government! An announcement was made that many personnel would be allowed an opportunity to retire early–with a cash bonus if one would *volunteer* for early retirement.

I was ready!

The only problem was that the offer applied only to non-supervisors–and, ironically, I was now the head of the section!

I asked around, and I was told that the only way I, as a supervisor, could retire early, was if the

Commanding General of Walter Reed would approve it himself—put his signature on my retirement papers, to override the general policy that he had already made.

As luck would have it, who do you suppose had become Commanding General of Walter Reed Army Medical Center? After all these years?

***

Remember, when I was a twenty-something Speech Pathologist, and two young Army doctors had carried me into a hospital room, ostensibly to treat ... a corpse? Yes, one of those young doctors, after a long and illustrious career in military medical administration, was now the Commanding General!

There had been a reception for General Blanck, when he was sworn in as our Commanding General. I had gone through the reception line to meet again my "friend"—the perpetrator of my introduction to the corpse! As I shook his hand, I asked whether he remembered me. Well, he soon remembered both me and that long-ago incident.

"Oh-h-h, please don't tell anyone about that," he had said, with a broad grin. "I owe you one."

So, now I "had something" on the Commanding General, and, by his own word, he "owed me one."

***

When I learned that General Blanck had the power to effect my early retirement, I filled out my retirement application, then took it to his office. He was not there, but his secretary allowed me to place my papers on his desk—with a note that read, in part:

"Dear General Blank, "You still owe me one ... ☺ ... and this is the one I want ☺."

Before long, I received notification–through official channels–that my retirement *was approved!*

A NEW BEGINNING

The very day that I announced my retirement to my unit–to my fellow speech pathologists–I happened to stop by my son Andrew's elementary school, New Hampshire Estates. I often dropped by there, for one reason or another, in support of the school's various programs.

At one point, I had initiated and co-chaired a Silent Auction, a PTA activity to raise money to provide supplemental funds for resources that were unavailable from public money.

At an earlier time, I had given two lectures at the school–one for the parents at an evening meeting of the PTA and one in the daytime for the teachers.

***

"Catch The Parent Being Wrong"

For the parents, I had spoken of how they could help their children's speech development at home, in everyday conversation. I told them this: "Play a game with your children, around the dinner table. Tell them that, if they catch you "mispronouncing" a word, a certain number of times, they will get a "star," and a certain number of stars will get them a trip to McDonalds–or some other reward that would appeal to your particular child."

For example, I told them,

"If your child is saying w for r (wabbit for rabbit), give him or her an example of some other "mispronunciation," such as "th" for "s"–but specifically avoid saying anything about the "w" for "r." The reason for avoiding the child's own specific problem sound is to avoid making the child feel that the parent is "making fun" or humiliating him/her. The parent should let the speech therapist teach the child the proper pronunciation (articulation) of the various letters and sounds. The home exercise is just to get the child in the habit of listening to himself as he/she speaks.

"Thus, instead of "catching" your child doing something wrong," I said, "you give your child permission to catch *you* doing something wrong. Kids *LOVE* catching adults being wrong! Especially, parents! Soon enough, they will start catching *themselves* being wrong, as well."

In Speech Pathology, we call this "ear training."

Another important point I stressed to parents is that, when talking with their child, especially about pronunciations, the parent should make sure that they are down at the level where the child can see the parent's mouth and lips as they converse. Otherwise, the child cannot see how the parent is making the sounds, and will be unable to copy it. Of course, there are many sounds that the child cannot see how you make them–such as the "k" and the "g,"–because the child cannot see the exact tongue placement through the partially closed lips. The "p" and the "b" and the "m" are usually learned first, because they are the sound placements that are the most visible. That is why most kids say "Ma-Ma" before they say "Da-Da"–the "m" sound is made with the lips, while the "d" sound is made with the tongue on the forward palate. You can see the "m" but you cannot see the "d."

Count The "Fs"

When I spoke to the teachers, as part of my lecture, I had given them a simple little "test." I said, "The object here is to test your alphabetic recognition skills. Read the following passage carefully; then without saying anything to anyone, write down the number of "Fs" you can count."

Test:

"Finished files are the result of years of scientific study, combined with the experience of years."

(Try it! Test yourself! How many "Fs" are there?)

After the test was over, we compared their individual counts of the number of Fs with the true number. As I expected, most of the teachers—just like any other group of normally intelligent adults—counted fewer than the correct number. (The correct number is six! How did you do?)

I said to the assembled group of certificated teachers, "Now, wait a minute. You are teaching reading, writing, and spelling here; you have my son in this school, and you can't recognize all of the letter "Fs" in a simple sentence?" I laid it on pretty thick, so as to make them feel pretty sheepish about it; I was really condescending. Finally, I said, "Please forgive me for being so condescending, but I wanted you all to experience, a little bit, how it feels to a kid with a speech problem (or, alternatively, a learning disability) to be talked down to or ridiculed."

"Let me show you how many "Fs" there are, and how easy it is *not* to find them all." I went through the sentence very slowly, carefully pointing out each letter "F" - including the two instances of the letter "F" in the word "of." Then I pointed out how easy it is to slide right by the word "of," because it is such a little, routine word. I also pointed out that the letter f in the word "of" is pronounced with a "v" sound, as if it were "ov." I believe that this may play a role in ignoring those two Fs, especially if one has a tendency to pronounce the words to oneself as one reads them. (You can bet that, when one is counting very carefully, as part of a test, any tendency to softly pronounce the words to oneself is increased.)

Then I said, "I want to assure you that your answers are definitely within normal limits. But now you know a little of what it feels like to have a learning disability—and *especially* to have someone *ridicule* you for it."

Several teachers approached me afterward to express their amazement at this clever little test, asking me for a copy of it, so they could play the same trick on their friends.

***

On this day, the day of my retirement announcement, on my way home from Walter Reed, I was stopping by the school to drop off some materials I had saved to contribute to the art teacher's arts and crafts activities. After leaving the art teacher's room, I chanced to meet the counselor, Lois Harris. She said, "Hi! What are you doing here?" I told her about the art supplies, then mentioned that I had just announced to my staff that I was retiring at the end of the month, September 30.

"Does Miss. B [the principal] know about this?"

"No, it just happened today."

"Do you mind if I tell her?"

"Not at all."

A few minutes later, as I was driving out of the parking lot, I chanced to see in my rear-view mirror a very white-haired woman, in high-heeled shoes, running frantically after my car, flailing her arms, waving desperately. (I can still see her, *in my rear view mirror*, to this day.) It was the School Principal, JoAnne Busalacchi ("Ms. B").

OMIGOD! I thought. *What have I done? Have I hit a kid? Or what?*

I stopped, and she caught up to me. Putting my window down, I heard her query me insistently: "Is it true?" she almost shouted, out of breath. "You've retired from Walter Reed? Is it true?"

"Yes," I said. "I just announced my retirement to my staff this afternoon."

"You've got to come *here*! You've *got* to *come!*"

"What in the world are you talking about?"

"We don't have a speech therapist for the year—and we're already two weeks into the term. You've got to come! You've just got to come!"

"Could I work just at this one school only?"

"Yes!"

"Can I work just three days a week?"

"Yes!"

And that was my interview! A month later, after a short breather, I began another career, at New Hampshire Estates Elementary School. That is to say that, after my 27 years at Walter Reed, I found myself resuming my *earliest* career, as an elementary-school speech therapist.

JoAnne Busalacchi

One measure of "Ms. B's" commitment to "her" kids was the energy and urgency of her recruitment sprint—when she recruited me in the parking lot, running after my car to beg me to take the open position in speech therapy at her school.

Whether I always agreed or not with what Ms. B did, I always knew that what she did was motivated entirely by her sense of what was the best for the good of her kids. She always had the interest of the kids at heart. She was very frank, very strong in her opinions, but she trusted and respected her people; in meetings with parents, she always let everyone speak. What is more, she was always alert to my coming in to work on a day for which I was not being paid!

PEANUT BUTTER SANDWICH

One of my speech therapy classes at New Hampshire Estates was a group of language-delayed kids. My language-delay class had four second-graders with an expressive language-delay disorder. They were not monitoring their own verbal output well enough to make corrections to what they were saying. They would just talk on and on, without knowing that they were not being understood or without understanding how they could change what they were saying to make themselves understood. It was not poor articulation (poor pronunciation)−rather it was a language problem−an inability to think of the right words, or the right word sequence, to make themselves understood *unambiguously.*

I always wanted my speech-therapy classes to be *fun* for the kids. That's why−when I was a very young school speech therapist−I decided to call it Speech Club instead of speech therapy. Kids do not want to be set apart or singled out as different, or deficient, even at a young age. So, when I went into a regular classroom to pick up my kids for their therapy session, I always announced myself by saying, "Time for Speech Club!" The designated kids−they knew who they were−would RUN to join me at the classroom door, maybe thinking, "What crazy thing is she going to do today?" I had contrived it to seem a special privilege.

Doing Speech Club again, near the end of my career, I remembered the little girl, Brenda, in Orangeville Illinois, who came back to school one fall, *faking* a W for R ("wabbit for rabbit") problem, because, as she admitted tearfully, "We had *so* much fun in Speech Club last year!"

This had one unintended down side though. Some of the other kids may have wondered or worried why they had not been selected for the *privilege* of Speech Club. I always remembered that, when I was in elementary school and my peers were called out of class to go to their speech therapy session, I felt left out, especially when I learned that they "played games" in speech therapy–while I was stuck back in the classroom, having to study *geography*! So, when I was a young "teacher," and later as a very mature one, I had some empathy for the kids who may have been jealous of *their* peers in Speech Club.

Getting back to my language-delay class, though–I wanted to invent some way to help each and all of them to start to monitor their own verbal output. I wanted to create an exercise that could help them and motivate them and, at the same time, that would be fun and had some reward at the end of it.

I thought, *What better reward for growing kids than peanut butter sandwiches?* Most of the kids at my recent school were on a free lunch program; many of their families were not well off. Not every kid came to this particular school having had a proper breakfast; some might already be hungry long before lunchtime.

These were not primarily ESOL (English for Speakers of Other Languages) kids. That is, they were not necessarily struggling with learning a *new* language. The kids for whom English was not their *primary* language would have been in my care only if they had the same language delay in their primary language that they had in English.

I went out from home, over the weekend, to get the component materials for peanut butter sandwiches: bread, peanut butter and a knife. Also, a jar of jelly—and paper plates.

In class, I started out: "We are going to have a treat today! We are going to make peanut butter sandwiches!"

"Yeay!" They immediately got excited. They could see the materials on the table, so—even though Speech Club was usually a moderately serious business—they knew I wasn't kidding. They could see peanut butter sandwiches were soon to be made.

"But you will have to help me! Give me some help. You will have to tell me how to do it!

I don't know for sure if they realized this was also going to be a learning exercise. In any case, I just kept playing dumb.

"Its easy!" they all chorused together.

"Well, tell me the first thing to do."

"Take the bread out!"

"Take - the - bread - out. OK, I get it. I can do that! Just a minute."

So, I tuck the loaf of bread under my arm, and then, saying brightly, "See you later!" I start for the door.

The kids start screaming, "NO, NO! Take the bread out! Take the bread OUT!"

"Wait a minute! You said to take the bread out. Isn't this the bread?"

"Yes."

"And isn't that the door? Isn't that the way *out*?"

"Ye-ess."

"OK. I'll go now."

"NO! Don't GO out; just take the BREAD out!"

(It was beginning to be pure chaos by this time.)

"How can I take the bread out without going out myself? I can't just throw it out the window! That doesn't make any sense. I'll just take the bread in my hands and walk it out."

(Now, total mayhem:)

"NO! TAKE the BREAD out! TAKE THE BREAD OUT! Don't GO out! Take the *BREAD* OUT!

One kid–Tai Lam–actually grabs me, wanting to restrain me physically from going out the door.

"DON'T GO OUT!"

"Didn't you just say 'Take the bread out?'"

They start talking animatedly among themselves about the crazy-dumb teacher. They don't know what to make of me–not able to understand their very, very simple instruction.

This was one of the happiest–one of the most exciting things, lessons, I ever did with my kids. No speech therapist that I ever knew ever did it, before or since, and I got such an incredible response from it, that I knew it was working.

Finally, an idea: "Take the bread out of the BAG!" one says, and they all start shouting together: "TAKE THE BREAD OUT OF THE *BAG*!, TAKE THE BREAD OUT OF THE *BAG*!"

Oh! I think I'm beginning to see. (Pause.) This is the bag. (Pause.) And this is the bread. (Pause.) So I need to take the bread...out...of the bag....

"OH! NOW I get it. Take - The - Bread (gesturing) ***OutOfTheBag!*** **Ohhh-*KAY*!** I can *do* that!"

I reach into the bag and grab as many slices as my hand will hold, and I start taking handful after handful out of the bag—stacking them up on the tabletop.

"NO! TOO MANY! Don't take it ALL out!" (Peals of ridiculing laughter.)

"How many?"

"Just one!"

"OK, just one. There! What's next?"

"Put it on the plate."

"Put WHAT on the plate?"

"The bread! The bread! Put the bread on the plate! The bread!"

I plop the bag, containing the remainder of the bread, squarely onto the plate.

"OK, there it is on the plate."

"NO-O! Not the whole bag! Just ONE SLICE!"

"OK...Just one slice. Is that right now"

"YE-ES! YE-ES! Now put the peanut butter on the bread."

"Oh! OK. I can do that! Thanks!" (Plop! I put the peanut butter jar squarely onto the slice of bread.)

"NO! NO! NO!" they all chorus (laughing hysterically.)

Now I can see them thinking, "This teacher is a moron! She Is R-e-a-l-l-y Dumb!"

"But...you <u>did</u> <u>say</u>..."Put The *Peanut Butter* [Pointing] On The *Bread* [Pointing]."

"Isn't that what you said? And isn't that what I did?"

There is a *long* silence—as I watch them digesting my words. There is *such* a silence...I can almost *hear* them processing my words.

Finally, one says, thoughtfully, "Not the whole jar."

"Not the whole JAR!" they all shout. (Another chorus of derisive, hysterical laughter.)

Kids love catching a grown-up in the wrong. Kids are always being told they are wrong. For once now, they are the experts, and they are seeing that the teacher, the adult in the room, is totally, catastrophically wrong. Through all their amazement and perplexity, I could see, hear, and feel their joy in finding me wrong...and telling me so.

"But, do you see why I did what I did?"

"Well...yeah....but...but...." one kid offers.

"You have to *open* the peanut butter!" another adds.

194

"What do you mean, '*Open* the peanut butter.' How do I *open* the peanut butter?"

"Take the top off!"

"Take what top off?"

"The top of the *jar*. Take the top of the *jar* off."

"Oh, I see...I can do that." I remove the lid. (Pause. Expectant look from me.)

"Get the peanut butter out of the jar."

I start to squeeze my hand into the top of the jar, as if I'm about to scoop up a handful of peanut butter. *I hope they stop me quick,* I think. *I don't want to contaminate this peanut butter*

"NO! NO! THE KNIFE! USE THE KNIFE!"

I make a gesture, as if wiping messy fingers on my apron, I pick up the knife and grab a dollop of peanut butter. "Now what?"

"Spread it on the bread...."

"Spread *what* on the bread?"

"THE PEANUT BUTTER! THE PEANUT BUTTER! PUT THE...WITH THE KNIFE...WITH THE KNIFE, PUT THE PEANUT BUTTER ON THE BREAD!! WITH THE KNIFE! WITH THE KNIFE!" they all chorus.

They were getting a big kick out of all this; they seemed both appalled and delighted, seeing their "teacher" playing (or being) dumb, while they were —for once in their school life—the smart ones. They would look at one another, almost with panic, thinking,

"What are we going to do?" But they were also nearly hysterical with laughter, at me.

Some stood right up out of their chairs, with arms flailing, desperately trying to push a thought into my brain—physically, if in no other way—substituting gross motor movement for the impulse to verbalize something, something that just wasn't working yet on the teacher's brain. Nothing was working out right. One kid climbed—shouting—right up on the seat of her chair....

Sigmund Freud said that strongly felt psychic energy has to come out, somehow. If it cannot come out directly, in conscious thought and audible verbalization, it will be *sublimated*; it will come out in some other way—maybe physically. Possibly violently!

With the peanut butter now spread onto the bread, I put both hands on my hips and ask, "Now What?"

"Put the jelly on the peanut butter."

I put the top back on the peanut butter, and slowly, carefully, start to position the jelly jar on top of the peanut butter jar.

"NO, NO, NO" they all shout, giggling wildly.

As this continues, I can see them beginning to monitor their verbal output. As we keep on, I am beginning to see the sentences getting longer, more complex. They are starting to use more words, erasing ambiguities. Also, they were starting to look more proud, feeling some new power in affecting their *teacher's* behavior. They would start to say something, start again, pause, wrinkle brows—look around at each other. I could see them starting to think. Slowly, haltingly, their brains were starting to process what they were about to say, *before they said it.* ("Be sure brain is in gear, before engaging ....") For the first time, I was seeing them taking the initiative to correct themselves. In *therapy-speak*, they were *self-correcting*. "Take the bread out... ... ...I mean, take it *out of the package*... ... take ONE SLICE! Take it out of the package...take *one slice* out of the package."

Their verbal gyrations had become something like trying to solve a verbal version of the Rubik's Cube. They experimented, first one way and then another. When one way didn't work, they would back up, think a moment, then try something else, until they began to get it right. Once one kid got it "right," their friends would light up: *Yes, that's right!* They would smile broadly and all begin repeating the phrase, shouting with boundless happiness.

A teacher seldom gets to see, so vividly, her students' learning actually entering their heads and coming back out as behavior. It was a trip!

This went on and on, through opening the jelly jar, spreading the jelly, adding a top slice of bread, and then repeating the whole process to produce a second sandwich.

As we kept on, I was seeing the sentences getting longer–more complex. They were using more words, erasing ambiguity. They were also amazingly involved. This was not like an ordinary classroom lesson–with them sitting and (maybe) listening (but surely fidgeting). This was SPEECH CLUB!

The proof of learning is that the second sandwich took barely half as long to complete as the first.

Finally, I cut each sandwich into two pieces and passed them around, each kid getting half a sandwich. No tea sandwiches for this group! They'd been working up an appetite for probably twenty minutes, doing the hard labor of schooling me in the mechanics of making lunch.

I don't think I provided anything to drink, unless it was just a cup of water. The kids were happy just to get their sandwich-reward and to start chowing down.

Now, you may be thinking, "What if some kid has a deadly food allergy involving peanuts? I thought of that—you bet! I had checked with the school nurse beforehand, to see if any of my four language-delayed kids were allergic to peanuts. You can be sure that no school nurse worth her salt, by the 1990s, would have shirked her duty of asking the allergy questions of the parent (or grandparent) who brought her kid to registration for school. *Not at New Hampshire Estates Elementary School; not under Principal JoAnne Busalacchi!*

TAI LAM

Early one Fall, Ms. McGinn spoke to me about a child, a little boy named Tai Lam, a child with behavioral concerns, in her 2nd grade class. She thought he was acting out because of his frustration at not being able to communicate his thoughts and his needs; his speech was virtually unintelligible. She said that he seemed really smart—he did very well with math problems—but his articulation was terrible. When things did not go his way, he would shut down and stop all participation. So I took Tai Lam into one of my speech therapy groups.

One morning, I was walking down the hallway to the all-purpose room, where kids were gathering for lunch. *What's this?* It was Tai Lam, sitting alone on the hallway floor, in the dim and otherwise-deserted hallway. He wouldn't get up from the floor. Other teachers came along and stood around, saying things like, "Come on Tai, get up." But Tai wouldn't get up. So I got down on the floor with him and said, "Tai, we can do this together; we'll get through this. I'm going to stay right here until you're ready to get up." I tried to put into words the frustration he must be feeling: "It must be very hard to have a lot of good ideas, and not be able to say them so that others can understand you. But this is going to get better, and we're going to work together until it does." The other teachers were drifting away. "I love you, Tai. I hate to see you shutting down like this." He finally began to calm down, and we went in together, for lunch.

Tai was a brilliant kid. He worked really hard with me, and I loved working with him. He came in, eager to work. And he never gave *me* a problem, as he had done elsewhere. I showed him how to use his mouth, where to put his tongue for the different speech sounds and so on. When I drilled him hard, I felt guilty; but I knew that it was for his benefit. As I drilled him again and again, I would sometimes purposely skip over one of the problem sounds, and he would say, "You missed one!" By the time his speech became 70 percent intelligible, I was learning just how very smart he was.

We don't know what things were like for Tai at home. We had meetings about him, but no parent ever came. In that neighborhood, typically, both parents likely would be working—often multiple jobs, to make ends meet—and could not easily take time off to attend daytime meetings at their children's schools. In any case, the school reported Tai's case to protective services (twice) for bruises. Once he started speech therapy with me, I remember Ms. McGinn saying, "He's really making progress in class." That made me feel really good. By the time he left New Hampshire Estates at the end of third grade, he was 100 percent intelligible.

Years later, I saw an afternoon TV report about a shooting at a bus stop. A group of young men had boarded a bus and began trying to provoke an argument. At another stop, that group got off the bus and one of them pulled out a gun and fired several shots back at a group of teenagers inside, while a second man held the bus's door from closing. Three kids inside the bus were wounded.

I learned a day later–when a teacher emailed me–that one of the wounded was Tai Lam. Tai was taken to a hospital, but he was gone.[43]

I was devastated. I knew that teachers and therapists were not supposed to have favorites among the kids they teach or treat. But honestly, I have to say, Tai was one of my most favorite students. He was a favorite because he really needed me, and I knew it; I knew I could help him, and as he worked with me I could see his intelligence. I knew I was making a difference. He would light up like a Christmas tree when he made a sound he hadn't been able to make before. And he would *run* in to "Speech Club," and be the first kid in the room. He would literally *run in to see me,* with a huge smile on his face! He was a genius-level kid. By the time he graduated from third grade and moved on to the nearby 4th-to-7th-grade school, I had seen him for about two years; he had become totally intelligible and a very manageable, very enjoyable boy.

In high school, following his older brother's influence, Tai had joined the wrestling team, in the 103-pound weight class. According to friends, he was also in the Fashion Club. He was a "stylish" freshman, who almost won the "best-dressed" award the year before.[44]

---

[43] "Hector Hernandez, 21, pleaded guilty to second-degree murder in the death of Tai Lam. State guidelines call for Hernandez to receive a sentence of between 15 and 45 years, prosecutors said." About a month before the Nov. 1 shooting, Hernandez had been arrested for possession of a switchblade knife and threatening a student at a nearby high school. His status as an alleged illegal immigrant went undetected at the time." –The Washington Post, May 1, 2009. Retrieved Feb. 14, 2015.

[44] "Silver Spring Teenager Fatally Shot On Md. Bus." –The Washington Post, Nov. 3, 2008.

The funeral was a mob scene, and they were accepting contributions for the burial. There were many, many students there. I learned, from those I talked to at the funeral, that Tai Lam had become, by the time he was in high school, one of the most popular kids at school. Everyone liked him. He was really making progress both academically and socially.

I waited a *very* long time in line to pay my respects to his mother. But the longer I waited, the more I realized that I had no words of comfort for her. My own grief, my own sense of lost potential and personal loss were such that I could only have added to hers. My heart breaking, I slipped quietly out of the line and drove tearfully home.

AN UNEXPECTED GIFT

"This is the answer to my prayers–I don't want anything done."

A minute before, my mother's physician had said, "Well, we've got a little cancer here."

"I don't want any chemo or radiation," said Mom; "I've had a wonderful life, but it's enough!"

The doctor turned to me and asked, "How do you feel about this?" "Well," I answered, "I think that when someone gets cancer it must feel like a complete loss of control over one's life and self. I want Mom to have all the control she can possibly have, so I will support whatever she decides."

Mom was 103. She had married a wonderful man (my father), raised three children, volunteered charitably all her life, traveled extensively and was a ferocious fan and knowledgeable critic of the opera. Following her husband's passing, with children long grown up, she had enjoyed more than thirty years of complete independence and financial security. There was little she had ever wanted that she hadn't possessed or done. But there were heartaches too.

I was born with the congenital spinal defect known as Spina Bifida. This was 1939. The day I was born, doctors told my parents to put me in an institution right away, before they could become emotionally attached to me. They said I would never walk or talk– that I'd be mentally handicapped and completely dependent.

Decades later I chanced to read, in Mom's diary of those days, that she cried all day, the day that I was born.

My parents chose to take me home.

As I grew up with special needs, Mom was the ultimate caregiver to me. She drove me to countless doctor's appointments. She washed and changed my bed sheets every day of my life for nine years, until I finally was able to gain control of my bladder. When I conceived a desire to be a "Brownie," and there was no Brownie scout troop available at the elementary school for handicapped children that I attended, she started and led a Brownie troop at my school. I never heard her complain about anything she did for me. Years later, when I wondered out loud how hard all that must have been for her, she replied, "What makes you think I didn't love taking care of you?"

I eventually earned a masters degree in Speech Pathology, and became the head of the Speech Pathology section at Walter Reed Army Medical Center, thanks in great part to the unfailing care, love, and support of my parents.

Towards the end of her life, Mom had fabulous hospice care, but she always seemed relieved when I came to see her. The night before she died, I knew that she was declining fast. I decided to sleep overnight in her living room. I had not been at my father's side when he died, and I did not want to be absent when Mom passed.

Early in the morning, she yelled out, "Pam, Pam!" I said "I'm here Mom." She said, "Oh good, 'cause I need you now." I said, "I'm here Mom, and I'm not going anywhere." She said "Oh good!" Those were her last words. I sat with her for the next six hours, holding her hand, until she took her last breath. I was so honored to be with her then.

So often, Mom would thank me profusely for helping her–getting her groceries, taking her out to lunch, sewing her clothes, getting her watch fixed, taking her to doctor's appointments–or just going to visit with her. My response was always, "I'm just returning a portion of what you did for me." I'm sure Mom didn't think about this in those early years, but in her exhaustive caregiving she had created her own caregiver: me.

I wouldn't be completely honest if I didn't admit that there were times when I felt it a burden–to put my own life essentially on hold as I would twice a week drive to her apartment, get her groceries and complete other tasks–but looking back now, I'm so thankful that I had the opportunity to return her caregiving, at the time she needed me most. Nothing was left unsaid or undone.

When I retired from New Hampshire Estates Elementary School, I became a potter. Among the pottery than I hand-made and hand-painted, I am especially fond of a plaque I made that reads, "Life is not about waiting for the storm to pass, it's about learning to dance in the rain." This thought, attributed to Vivian Greene,[45] aptly summarizes a life-view that I learned from my mother, who made "a wonderful life" for herself and her family, without dwelling on whatever rain or tears came into it.

That thought got me through the rough times– times that are inevitable when you're caring for someone you love so much. Caregiving taught me much more than I ever expected–but not only about my mother and myself. I also learned about the feeling of

[45] –http://www.viviangreene.com/

fulfillment that comes with caregiving. I've learned that end-of-life caregiving can be an opportunity to gain a sense of completion in one's relationship with the person for whom one is caring. I've learned, after spending a significant time caregiving for someone I greatly love, that my grieving process has been so much smoother and easier than when I lost loved ones for whom I was not lucky enough to have been their personal caregiver.

This was an unexpected gift.

MY "FINAL CAREER"

Once the word got around New Hampshire Estates Elementary School that I was retiring (again), two of my teacher-colleagues, almost on the same day but completely unknown to each other, suggested to me that I should try my hand at pottery. They were both working, in their spare time, doing pottery at the Langley Park Community Center. Well, I thought, I could look into it. So, I looked into it, and I wound up doing pottery at the Center for about 12 years!

The Langley Park Community Center was a wonderful place to learn and to create pottery. The Center had several pottery wheels, TWO kilns, and about 40 carefully maintained pots of glaze in a multitude of colors. So I never had to buy and keep any of those at home, with the attendant mess, cost and space requirements–not to mention the time that would have been required of me to maintain all of that. Instead, I just paid a periodic fee to take the "class," which provided a teacher on premises for the one day a week I attended "class"–plus unlimited access to the pottery studio and all of its resources every day. Since I was now retired from all employment, I was free to use the unlimited access in an unlimited way; I was there every morning, as if it were a seven-day-a-week job. If anyone ever invited me to anything to which I didn't want to go, I just said that I had to be at the studio, which I referred to as "my job and my religion."

It was not an easy skill to learn, but what I loved so much about it was that I could paint on my pottery pieces, with colored "under-glazes," before their final firings.

Thus, I learned to create functional art, attractive objects with which to fill one's home, that one could actually use: teapots and bowls, casseroles, soap dishes, spoon rests, plaques, vases, platters, serving trays, candlesticks, sconces–all of which, when finished, were dishwasher-, oven-, and microwave-safe (as well as lead-free), making them very suitable for everyday use as well as attractive for special occasions, artistic display, and gifts.

I had always longed to create art, but I was very inhibited from thinking of myself as an artist; it seemed that I was never among those whose "picture" the teacher would choose to display on the wall. Now, as an adult, I found that I loved making these artistic things that one could use, and that other people appreciated and would pay for, to display in their homes!

When I did my first show and realized that people would actually buy my stuff–not only offsetting my expenses but providing a profit–I was hooked! Nevertheless, I was having so much fun making the stuff that I was accumulating more inventory than I was getting rid of. I needed to find more outlets for my product, so I could keep on working and having fun at the studio.

That was when I got into having shows in my home and selling my pottery for funds to support my charities. The first such occasion was inspired by the 2004 tsunami in Asia, when hundreds of thousands of people were overwhelmed and drowned or left "missing" by an enormous "tidal wave," caused by an undersea earthquake. The next year, 2005. was the occasion of Hurricane Katrina, which wreaked great devastation to the New Orleans and Baton Rouge regions.

A few months after my Hurricane Katrina sale, David received in the mailbox a solicitation to donate cash to The Smile Train—the nonprofit organization through which many doctors and other medical personnel volunteer their vacation time to travel to poorer countries to perform cleft-palate surgeries on children of families who otherwise would be unable to afford such life-changing therapy. David immediately recognized the relationship between the work of the Smile Train and the work I had done with the Cleft Palate Clinic at Walter Reed. It was indeed a no-brainer, and we soon found ourselves organizing another pottery sale in our home for The Smile Train.

David helped, among other ways, by designing, printing and posting on telephone poles all around our neighborhood, colorful posters promoting each of our periodic sales. Meanwhile, Andrew would help me set up tables and arrange the pottery for its most advantageous display. Various friends would volunteer their help—for instance in cashiering and in wrapping purchases into packages for carrying home. For refreshments to be offered to buyers, I bought cookies from Costco and solicited donations of food and drink from Starbucks, Dunkin' Donuts, and Domino's Pizza.

Our first charitable sale, for the tsunami, had realized about $1,400. For Katrina we collected and donated even more. And for the Smile Train, we had a sale every year for a few years, which enabled donations totaling about $5,000! Not only that, but I carefully withheld my donations until after the Smile Train would periodically announce a two-for-one match of all donated funds, thereby trebling the effect of our donations.

Since the Smile train estimated that each $250 would support the expenses for one cleft-palate surgery, our work on behalf of poor kids in other countries ultimately subsidized sending, in all, about 60 kids to surgery—radically changing their lives, to the benefit of their entire extended families and social-economic environments.

Eventually, as we prepared to move to the Riderwood Village Continuing Care facility in Silver Spring, Maryland, I decided that I had given the last benefit in my home. But then, there was a devastating earthquake in Haiti, just a couple of months after my "last" benefit. I decided that I had to "strike while the iron was hot," and immediately give another benefit for Haiti, while Haiti was on everyone's minds. So we were able to make about another thousand dollars for Haiti—which we sent to Doctors Without Borders, earmarked for Haiti.

A Thank You from The Smile Train.

OWNING MY SUCCESSES

All my life, I've made excuses—not for my failures but for my successes. On one hand, I always tried to hide my handicap, telling literally *no one* of how I was born or the history of my development. On the other hand, my handicap was always in my mind as a ready explanation *to myself*—anything but actual *merit*—for my every accomplishment. I did a good job of hiding my handicap from others, but I couldn't "hide" it from me. Whenever I was complimented for something, whenever I was chosen for something over others, I quietly thought to myself, *She only said that because I'm handicapped*, or *They're just being nice to me; they only chose me because I walk funny*. (It's true!)

One facet of being born not quite normal, and not quite up to the usual standard, is that I have an inordinate need to "prove" myself. I've already told the story of how I got myself so worked up over my mother's coming to visit, having the house perfect and such—even though I was taking a four-week, full-time course at the time to become a trainer for the Leadership and Management Development course for the U.S. Army—that I developed a case of the hives. Well, that was just an extreme case of the anxiety I get into EVERY time I entertain. The House, the food, the everything has to be perfect. I have to prove *every time* that I am not a poor little handicapped girl, unable to cope with keeping up my household, etc. etc. (That's true.) If someone entertains me for dinner at their house, with pizza and breadsticks, I have to reciprocate with dinner at my house, serving Beef Wellington and Cherries Jubilee! (So true.)

I've been thinking a lot lately about "owning" my successes. I mean, I recently realized that, through my life, I never really credited myself with any of my accomplishments. I realize now that I have credited my every success in life to others' sympathy over my handicap! I believed that I got to do all of those things because people felt sorry for me! For instance, in my first year at Illinois State Normal University, I was elected Secretary of the Freshman Class—after someone else suggested I run and really *pushed* me into doing it—and of course I figured it was out of sympathy. As a sophomore, I was voted one of the "Ten Best Dressed" on campus—on a "sympathy vote," I was sure. As a Senior, I was elected Co-Chair of the Big Four Dance Committee—the group that each year produced four major social dance events. Need you ask what I thought of that? I even believed I was allowed to graduate from college because of my handicap! I mean, I sort of believed that the professors fudged my grades upward, because they felt sorry for me!

Try to imagine this dialogue, of high school sorority girls in their membership meeting: "Let's let Pam in; she walks funny, we can help her!" There certainly was nobody who would have said that! I'm guessing now that they didn't notice my walk, or if they did, they noticed more my pitching in at the rush party, cutting up vegetables, or washing dishes, or asking, "What else can I do to help?" That's more likely to be—I realize now—what caused them to think, "She's one of us."

My husband would say that they were responding to my "charisma." David is the first and only person who ever described me as "charismatic." I haven't yet accepted his genial view, but I'm working on it. With David's help, I do begin to look back on my life and think, *Wow! I sure have done a lot of stuff! I didn't get to do all of that just because I'm handicapped...did I?*

Toward the end of my career at Walter Reed, I was appointed Supervisor of the Speech/Language Pathology Section. But, secretly, I couldn't accept that I was chosen for my competence. I thought, again, that it was all about sympathy for my "handicap." Never mind that—of the group—I was the most senior. Never mind that I had taken a week-long training course in Leadership and Management Development. Never mind that, at the end of *that* course, I was *chosen* to take, and did take, a *month-long* course—learning to become a *trainer* for the Leadership and Management Development course. Never mind that I co-taught the course to civilian officials well above my rank, as well as to numerous high Army officers, up to the rank of full Colonel.

I wonder if other people, living with a handicap, do that to themselves. Do they negate their achievements? Or do they let themselves think that they deserve, that they actually *earned* the rewards of their accomplishments? I wonder.

Now that we've moved to Riderwood Village, a huge senior living community in Silver Spring, Maryland, it seems that a lot of people here want to be my friend. Here—where many residents walk with canes or walkers, or ride powered wheelchairs—should I be thinking, *They saw my funny walk, and they figured "She'll fit right in!"*?

There has never been a day in my life that I could forget about my Spina Bifida. For example, I was reminded of my condition every time I went to the toilet–because I had to be very careful to use special techniques, that I had developed and taught myself, in order to fully empty my bladder. But I couldn't tell my story to anyone; I was too embarrassed. Ever since I left the Gompers school for the handicapped and entered a normal, regular high school, my lifelong obsession has been to hide my handicap. I needed to fit in, and my thinking was always dominated by the conviction that I never did fit in—or at least by the *fear* that I would not fit in.

But after a long and eventful life, I finally realize that *my identity is not defined by my Spina Bifida!* Could it be, considering all my accomplishments, that I should stop the denial? Should I begin to look at my gifts and accomplishments and stop thinking, in effect, *All that I am, or ever hope to be, is because I walk funny?!*

STEPPING AWAY FROM MY SHAME

One morning recently, I awoke with a new insight. After decades of dodging, I realized that all the hiding, all the shame I had felt about my Spina Bifida, was similar to the irrational guilt or shame that many rape survivors feel. Rape survivors are no more responsible for their rape than I am for the way I was born–with a hole in my spine. Perhaps the two feelings are similar; they both amount to taking on to oneself a burden of shame touching on a condition for which one is not responsible.

In parts of some countries, to this day, blaming the victim is ingrained in the culture. In such cultures–if you can believe it–it is considered the duty of the father or brothers of a girl who has been raped, to kill–not the rapist, but the *victim* of the rape–to "redeem the family's *honor!*" Such is the crazy, twisted morality of some cultures.

Even in our culture, it remains possible for the recipient of a random condition of birth to be blamed for it–and to blame and denigrate herself/himself. I wonder how many others, handicapped in some way, feel shame or guilt for their condition or for the special consideration, real or imagined, that others may afford them.

Of course, many handicaps are more plainly evident than mine. Beyond a slight limp (or "walking funny") my handicap was usually invisible. Yes, in my early years, especially, occasional bladder incontinence constantly threatened exposure by an accident out in public. But, almost every day of my life, I could pull off a reasonable imitation of a fully normal person. It was that appearance of normality that I sought to achieve, maintain and to protect *at all costs.*

Once, in high school, I stood talking to a group of boys, after school. In those days, girls wore "circle" skirts, that were billowed outward by one or more crinoline half-slips, each held at the waist either by an elastic waistband or by one or two hooks or "snaps." On this occasion, as I talked and perhaps flirted with the boys, my snap or hook broke, and I became gradually aware that my half-slip was slipping, slipping–ever downward. I didn't know what to do. If it slipped far enough to become obvious, I was going to be humiliated. Well, it kept slipping, until I could stand it no longer. I hurriedly excused myself from the group, and as I hastily retreated, running faster and faster, the slip kept slipping downward, faster and faster, until it hobbled me right around the ankles. Still in some kind of denial, I actually kept going! Finally, I got to my car, stepped out of the slip, snatched it up and fled from my living nightmare.

I burst through the front door, crying frantically to my mother, "We've got to move! Mother, we've got to move!"

"Whatever are you talking about, Pam?" said my mother–entering from the kitchen, drying hands on a towel. "What has happened?

I quickly told Mother, through my tears, what had happened. "I can't ever go back to that school! Oh; I'm so ashamed!" Then I told her what had happened.

Resourceful as always, my mother took me in her arms and said, "Of course you can go back, my dear. You just need some words to make a joke of it; then they will laugh *with* you, not *at* you."

So, the next day, when I saw the same boys again, and they began to refer to the previous day's scene, I just used the words my wise mother had supplied. I said, with a tauntingly assertive smile, "Well—where were the pennies? I thought you'd throw pennies for that performance! Where were the pennies?"

And with that, the whole embarrassing scene was turned into a memory that we could all laugh about together. My loving and capable mother had saved the day! I went on to graduate from Morgan Park High School; I never thought again about moving, with my whole family, away from the locale of my mortification.

I tell this story to show the measure of panic I could feel, my overwhelming fear of becoming an object of ridicule—whether for a scene of social embarrassment that could have happened to any teenaged girl of the time, or for my more unusual and intensely dreaded divergence from "normality," my Spina Bifida.

I'm not sure I have made it quite clear yet—*why* I felt such *shame* for my Spina Bifida (and its attendant incontinence) that I generalized my shame to situations that could have happened to anyone. Why did I so desperately need to seem normal, *even super-normal*, in every way.

Hiding my condition seemed more indispensible to me than perhaps it might be for a person without limbs—an amputee perhaps—with a back story of bravely defending his or her country's highest values. Why did I feel such *compulsion* to hide my condition?

Simply put, *babies* wet their pants!

Imagine the long road I have traveled, to the place where I am now telling my story for all the world to read!

I now feel *connected* to all the physically handicapped in a new way. Most of those confined to wheelchairs do not have the option of hiding their disability. It is out in front, for all to see. I wonder if they, too, sometimes feel shame or guilt for their condition, or for receiving special consideration, real or imagined. If so, that would be no more rational than the shame I felt for my Spina Bifida; or that some rape survivors feel for their rape; or that some homosexuals and transgendered individuals may have been made to feel for the way that *they* were born.

I fervently hope that, before I die, science will have found proof-positive that homosexuality and ambiguous gender are genetically determined, rather than some kind of choice, subject to moral judgment. I have too many good, gay friends to feel otherwise.

My chains have been broken now. I want everyone to know–as I have finally *come* to know–that *your handicap is not you, and you are not your handicap. Your rape is not you, nor are you your rape.* You are a human being–a child of God. Your moral worth is up to you; it depends on how sensitively you share this planet with your fellow creatures; no condition of your birth can count against your moral worth. You must know that I have felt the shame that you have felt—and I wish for you: peace, the knowledge that *you are you*, regardless of whatever *has happened to you* that was out of your control or choice. May you forever stop the hiding—the reluctance to share yourself and to be seen as you really are. May you gain and hold the self-assurance to speak of your condition—not as an identity joined to you, not as a reason for shame, but as merely a story among many that describe your experience, without reaching who you are or what you deserve in life.

EPILOGUE: *SHE WILL NOT GROW OUT OF IT !*

If you've come this far in my book, it may be because, somewhere along the way, you started rooting for me. If you've managed to stick with even the *boring* details of my life, even the little story of my learning to crochet, for example, maybe you've begun to realize that, when you take my exciting episodes together with the dull, I've somehow actually managed to live a normal life–unusual perhaps, but *normal.* That's great, because what I've wanted all my life, more than anything else, is to be *normal.* Praise be, I am. Normal, that is. *Who would have thought...?*

In all, I learned from my own life–and those of my patients and students–that great things may happen, if you hope and try; that pediatricians and surgeons (even speech-language pathologists) sometimes don't *know,* and when they *don't* know, they may sometimes just make something up, or tell you something that their professor made up, years ago. First, they may tell you something so pessimistic that it demolishes all your hope ("She'll never walk or talk.") when hope is everything to you. Or, second, they may tell you something so optimistic ("He'll grow out of it.") that it lulls you into complacency–into waiting till the child is older, when a completely successful intervention may be impossible. Between these opposites, medical or paramedical professionals may sometimes advise intervention that is ill-advised. ("Put her in an institution, before you get attached.") As a parent, educator, counselor, minister, priest, rabbi, imam, social worker, attorney, or advocate, it is *your job* both to *hope* and to *do*–never letting either down for the sake of the other; it is *your job* to get second opinions.

Sometimes, even with "good" advice, you may still prayerfully have to say the equivalent of: "No, she's part of our family; *she's coming home with us!*" Your daughter (or son, or patient, or student, or client or parishioner, or plaintiff or defendant) is *depending* on you for that.

I wish you all the help of Heaven and earth with these all-important decisions.

A WORD ABOUT MY TITLE

The meaning of my title–*She Will NOT Grow Out Of It !*–is twofold. First, it relates to a comment that I heard way too often, when speaking to parents of a child who should have had speech therapy years sooner, and which child's prognosis now for a completely successful intervention is poor: **"My pediatrician said she/he would grow out of it."** I wish I had a dollar for every time I've heard that. I sometimes want, in my imagination, to scream at those doctors, "He/she will NOT grow out of it!" While some children may grow out of some speech delays or deficits, most pediatricians were never trained to make such judgments, certainly not on the fly without a professional speech pathologist's evaluation.

Second, the title refers ironically (in reverse) to my own situation–comparing the way I was born to the way I eventually developed. At birth, doctors told my parents to put me into an institution, because I'd never walk or talk and I'd be "mentally retarded." In other words, I'd "never grow out of it." Contrary to the doctors' predictions–with fabulous parenting, a few well-timed surgeries and some luck–I did perfectly OK.

DEDICATION AND THANK YOU

For all those service people who are still missing, or who came home to mend and resume their lives—or to be buried. For special children and their educators. For all parents everywhere.

Somehow, I've always wanted to leave the world better than I found it. I've wanted not just to absorb and enjoy the resources of the world, but to add something of value to it. That's a pretty big ambition for someone of whom so little was expected, at birth. Whatever I've been able to accomplish, it would not have been possible without two very special people. Therefore...

A special thank you to: Ralph James Silverwood (1904-1978) and Kathryn Moore ("Tata") Silverwood (1907-2011)—the best parents on the planet! Without their support, without their love, hope and faith, their guidance, patience and perseverance—my life would have been totally different.[46]

---

[46] A statistical analysis of 84 adults living in the 21sr Century with Spina Bifida Myelomeningocele has been published as: "Adult Consequences of Spina Bifida: A Cohort Study." See References for a complete citation.

Mom and Dad, retired in Florida.

REFERENCES

"Adult Consequences of Spina Bifida: A Cohort Study." James W. Roach, MD; Barbara F. Short, RN and Hanna M. Saltzman. Clin. Orthop. Relat. Res. May 2011; 469(5): 1246–1252. Published online September 28, 2010; Retrieved April 12, 2017. ⁻https://www.ncbi.nlm.nih.gov/pmc/articles/PMC3069 297/#

As I Recall, Kathryn Moore Silverwood (self published). 115 p., ill. No date.

Before They Were The Packers, Green Bay's Town Team Days, Dennis J. Gullickson & Carl Hanson. Black Earth, WI, Trails Books. 2004. 294 p.

Eisenhower the President, Stephen Ambrose, 1984.

Microbe Hunters, Paul DeKruif, 1926

The Doctors Who Conquered Yellow Fever, Ralph Nading Hill, 1957.

Walter Reed–Doctor in Uniform, L. N. Wood., 1943.

NOTES

Made in the USA
Middletown, DE
08 May 2017